Captain Jinks of the Horse Marines a Fantastic Comedy in Three a cts

Clyde Fich

Copyright © BiblioLife, LLC

BiblioLife Reproduction Series: Our goal at BiblioLife is to help readers, educators and researchers by bringing back in print hard-to-find original publications at a reasonable price and, at the same time, preserve the legacy of literary history. The following book represents an authentic reproduction of the text as printed by the original publisher and may contain prior copyright references. While we have attempted to accurately maintain the integrity of the original work(s), from time to time there are problems with the original book scan that may result in minor errors in the reproduction, including imperfections such as missing and blurred pages, poor pictures, markings and other reproduction issues beyond our control. Because this work is culturally important, we have made it available as a part of our commitment to protecting, preserving and promoting the world's literature.

All of our books are in the "public domain" and some are derived from Open Source projects dedicated to digitizing historic literature. We believe that when we undertake the difficult task of re-creating them as attractive, readable and affordable books, we further the mutual goal of sharing these works with a larger audience. A portion of BiblioLife profits go back to Open Source projects in the form of a donation to the groups that do this important work around the world. If you would like to make a donation to these worthy Open Source projects, or would just like to get more information about these important initiatives, please visit www.bibliolife.com/opensource.

THE FIRST ACT

THE LANDING DOCK OF THE CUNARD LINE—*Late in the morning. The side of the vessel is seen on the left, with the passengers' gang-plank coming down to the centre of the stage. Across the river at the back is seen Hoboken with the Steevens house on the hill. It is a gray misty day, with a drizzling rain which flatters the Jersey shore. The paraphernalia of a landing stage is littered about, and some small groups of luggage arrived on the steamer have not yet been removed. A* Sailor *stands at the top of the gang-plank keeping a bored guard. There is a* Newsboy *selling the* Herald, Tribune, Times, Sun, Express, *and* Clipper. *A tired* Steward *now and then passes in sight on the boat. A* Policeman *walks in and out on the dock. It is raining and every one enters with a wet umbrella. The* Newsboy *sitting on a barrel is whistling "Captain Jinks" and kicking his heels against the barrel; he offers the* Policeman, *each time he passes him, a different paper. All the passengers except* Madame TRENTONI *have long ago left the boat. Several truckmen and loafers are more or less busy on the premises.*

CAPTAIN JINKS

PETER [*whistling, interrupts himself as the* Policeman *passes*]. Herald? [*The* Policeman *pays no attention to the boy at any time.* PETER *always continues whistling at once when he gets no answer, and continues the tune exactly where he left it off. The* Policeman *repasses*]. *Tri*-bune? Express? [*He continues whistling. The* Policeman *repasses.*] Times? [*Continues whistling.* Policeman *repasses.*] World? Clipper? [*Continues whistling as the* Policeman *passes out of sight.*]

The Tribune Reporter *hurries in. He goes quickly to the gang-plank and starts to walk up it. The* Sailor *at the top calls down and stops him.*

THE SAILOR. Nobody ain't allowed on board. [*The* Newsboy *laughs and whistles pointedly,* "*Shoo Fly, don't bother me!*"]

THE TRIBUNE REPORTER. Why not? I'm from the Tribune.

THE SAILOR. That don't make no difference, not if you was Boss Tweed from Tammany Hall!

THE TRIBUNE REPORTER. Madame Trentoni hasn't left the boat yet, has she?

THE SAILOR. There ain't no blamed Italyan on this yere boat!

THE TRIBUNE REPORTER. The young lady speaks English. I mean the great—

CAPTAIN JINKS
OF
THE HORSE MARINES

A FANTASTIC COMEDY IN THREE ACTS

BY CLYDE FITCH

NEW YORK
DOUBLEDAY, PAGE & COMPANY
1902

Copyright, 1902, by Doubleday, Page & Company
Published April, 1902

To V. G.
IN GRATEFUL APPRECIATION
OF A NEVER FAILING
SYMPATHY WITH AND UNDERSTANDING
OF ALL MY WORK
AND PLAY

New York, 1902

ILLUSTRATIONS

Miss Ethel Barrymore as *Aurelia Johnson* —
"*Madame Trentoni*" *Frontispiece*

Facing page

Sketch by Percy Anderson for *Madame Trentoni* 12

Aurelia. I'll tell you a secret· I want the big *crowd* to love me! I want to win the hearts of the gallery boys! 27

Mrs. Stonington. I am told the heroine is a — young person — no better than she should be, in fact not so good 46

Sketch by Percy Anderson for *Miss Merriam* 60

Sketch by Percy Anderson for the *Second Ballet Lady* 76

Aurelia. But I'm *nobody*.
Captain Jinks. The woman I love — *nobody?* 82

Sketch by Percy Anderson for the *Fourth Ballet Lady* "*Miss Hochspitz*" 86

Aurelia. Papa Belliarti and I are very happy! 92

Aurelia. We're all going to try our very best, aren't we, to-night?
The Sixth Ballet Lady [*the widow*]. Oh, it'll be hall roight. There ain't no trouble with that polka step! 96

Sketch by Percy Anderson for the *Sixth Ballet Lady* "*Mrs. Maggitt*" 102

Sketch by Percy Anderson for the *Sixth Ballet Lady's* Child — *Miss Victoria Alberta Maggitt* 108

Sketch by Percy Anderson for the *Seventh Ballet Lady* "*Mlle. Rosalie*" 118

ILLUSTRATIONS

AURELIA. Excuse me, gentlemen, but I can't have my rehearsal interrupted. Continue, Mrs. Gee. Now, ladies, please watch me!   124

SKETCH BY PERCY ANDERSON for *Mrs. Greenborough*   140

PROFESSOR BELLIARTI [*softly*]. Shall I make a little speech for you, dearie, and say you thank them all, and want them to have a happy evening?   152

THE FIRST ACT
[THE END OF OCTOBER]
The Landing Dock of the Cunard Steamship Company in New York

THE SECOND ACT
[A FORTNIGHT LATER]
Madame Trentoni's Parlor in the Brevoort House

THE THIRD ACT
[THE SAME NIGHT]
Still at Madame Trentoni's in the Brevoort House

TIME AND PLACE
New York City in the Early Seventies

The Costumes were designed by Percy Anderson and from Godey's Ladies' Book

The Play was Produced under the Management of Charles Frohman

PERSONS
CONCERNED IN THE PLAY

CAPTAIN ROBERT CARROLTON JINKS
CHARLES LA MARTINE
AUGUSTUS BLEEKER VON VORKENBURG
Professor BELLIARTI
The HERALD *Reporter*
The TRIBUNE *Reporter*
The TIMES *Reporter*
The SUN *Reporter*
The CLIPPER *Representative*
A Newsboy
An Official Detective
A Sailor
A Policeman
A Telegraph Boy
    Sailors, Domestics, and NEW YORKERS

MADAME TRENTONI (AURELIA JOHNSON)
MRS. GREENBOROUGH
MRS. JINKS
MRS. STONINGTON
MISS MERRIAM
1st Ballet Lady (MISS PETTITOES)
2nd Ballet Lady
3rd Ballet Lady
4th Ballet Lady (FRAULEIN HOCHSPITZ)
5th Ballet Lady
6th Ballet Lady (MRS. MAGGITT)
7th Ballet Lady
MARY: MADAME TRENTONI'S *Maid*

AS ORIGINALLY PRODUCED

At the WALNUT STREET THEATRE, Philadelphia, January 7, 1901, and at the GARRICK THEATRE, New York, February 4, where it played through the entire Season, and was revived for the beginning of the next.

CAPTAIN ROBERT CARROLTON JINKS	H. Reeves Smith
CHARLES LA MARTINE	George W. Howard
AUGUSTUS BLEEKER VAN VORKENBURG	H. S. Tabor
Professor BELLIARTI	Edwin Stevens
The HERALD *Reporter*	John R. Sumner
The TRIBUNE *Reporter*	Charles Marriott
The TIMES *Reporter*	Harry E. Asmus
The SUN *Reporter*	William Barstow Smith
The CLIPPER *Representative*	Gardner Jenkins
A Newsboy (PETER)	John Hughes
An Official Detective	Lewis Wood
A Sailor	Lorenzo Hale
A Policeman	M. J. Gallagher
A Telegraph Boy	Harry Barton
Sailors, Domestics, and NEW YORKERS	
MADAME TRENTONI (AURELIA JOHNSON)	Ethel Barrymore
MRS. GREENBOROUGH	Estelle Mortimer
MRS. JINKS	Mrs. Thomas Whiffen
MRS. STONINGTON	Fanny Addison Pitt
MISS MERRIAM	Sidney Cowell
1st Ballet Lady (MISS PETTITOES)	Lillian Thurgate
2nd Ballet Lady	Margaret Dunn
3rd Ballet Lady	Evelyn Jepson
4th Ballet Lady (FRAULEIN HOCHSPITZ)	Anita Rothe
5th Ballet Lady	Anna Morrison
6th Ballet Lady (MRS. MAGGITT)	Kate Ten Eyck
7th Ballet Lady	Alice Bryan
MARY	Beatrice Agnew

THE FIRST ACT

CAPTAIN JINKS

PETER [*stopping whistling to interrupt*]. Say, Jack! He means the Primy Donner what the young Prince of Wales says is a A one-er.

THE SAILOR. Oh, you mean the Opry Singer! She'll be leaving soon now. There's a good deal o' motion in her cabin, and there's eight men ordered below a struggling with her bag-gage.

THE TRIBUNE REPORTER [*eagerly, and with commendable zeal*]. How much baggage has she?

THE SAILOR. I dunno.

The Tribune Reporter *comes back down the gangplank.*

PETER [*on the barrel*]. Have the *Tri*-bune?

THE TRIBUNE REPORTER [*grandiloquently, feeling very much the importance of his position, especially as there is no other reporter there*]. *I* am the Tribune! [*He opens his umbrella and places it on the floor to dry.*]

PETER [*who is uneducated*]. Huh?

THE TRIBUNE REPORTER. *I* make the paper.

PETER. Where's your machine?

THE TRIBUNE REPORTER [*pointing to his forehead*]. Here!

PETER. Gee! I guess you're off your nut, ain't you?

CAPTAIN JINKS

THE TRIBUNE REPORTER [*obtusely*]. No, no, my boy. I'm a reporter.

PETER. All right, boss, but you ain't the only party what's after Miss Squeeler in there!

THE TRIBUNE REPORTER [*with supreme elegance*]. Other gentlemen of the Press, I presume?

PETER. Naw, it ain't no gentlemen—it's a big toff—a regular lardy-dah! what's been down here twice already with a gang of dandies and a brass band! The band was real discouraged the second time—was playing "Hail, Columbia" for all she was worth!

THE TRIBUNE REPORTER. I know about that. The Herald man got on to it yesterday. Hello, Times!

As the Times Reporter *comes on.*

THE TIMES REPORTER. Is she out yet?

THE TRIBUNE REPORTER. No. But look here, Captain Jinks has been here with his chums and a band in their uniforms straight from the Republican Parade.

THE TIMES REPORTER. If those fellows get hold of her first, we boys won't have a chance at an interview.

THE TRIBUNE REPORTER. Are they coming back?

PETER. Well, the band was a kickin', but I guess the swells'll be back, because they was full of bokays.

CAPTAIN JINKS

THE TRIBUNE REPORTER. They had a tug engaged to go over the bar to meet the boat to-morrow. Nobody ever dreamed she'd be in before. Think of crossing the ocean in fourteen days—it's a record-breaker! Mapleson calmly went on to Boston to come back to-night, or he'd be fixing everything for us!

THE TIMES REPORTER. I tell you what, we'll go get the boys now, quick, so we can all have a fair show together, and leave this youngster to tell Captain Jinks and his crowd when they come back that the lady won't— [*Interrupted.*]

PETER. She ain't no common *lady*, she's a Opry Singer what the Prince of Wales— [*Interrupted.*]

THE TRIBUNE REPORTER. Yes, yes! Mapleson gave us that story weeks ago. You tell Captain Jinks that Madame Trentoni won't leave the boat till after lunch. Are you fly?

PETER. What's it worth?

THE TIMES REPORTER. What'll you take?

PETER. You make *me* an offer.

THE TRIBUNE REPORTER. We'll give you a quarter. [*The* Newsboy *gives the* Tribune Reporter *one look, and then sticking his thumbs in the armholes of his waistcoat, he whistles "Shoo Fly, don't bother me!"*] Well, what's the matter?

CAPTAIN JINKS

PETER. You get some one else to do your job. I go to Sunday-school, an' I don't tell lies for nothing.

THE TIMES REPORTER. We'll give you a dollar.

PETER. All right! Pay in advance?

THE TRIBUNE REPORTER. Not by a long shot! Collect on delivery—of the lie! I'll go after the men, Jimmie, and you hang around out of the way here—just to keep an eye on the boy and see he *does his work!* [*Picking up his umbrella he goes out on to the street.*]

PETER. Gee! Lyin' 's no work fur me—it's play! That there about going to Sunday-school was a sample.

THE TIMES REPORTER. Look out! Here they come. [*Goes outside by the boat.*]

Three men are heard singing "Captain Jinks of the Horse Marines," faintly, then more loudly as they approach and come on through the big doorway on the right. The three men are CHARLIE, GUSSIE, *and* Captain JINKS. *They are good-looking young dandies,* GUSSIE *being more of a fop than the others,* Captain JINKS *himself having a superb figure and a frank handsome face. All he needs is one lesson to make a fine man of him. The three march in arm in arm,* Captain JINKS *in the centre. They wear scarlet uniforms and big bearskin caps. Each carries*

CAPTAIN JINKS

a bouquet of the period, small, with a flounce of lace around it. Their singing and marching is of course simply a joke among themselves. The Policeman *meets them coming from the opposite side.*

THE POLICEMAN. Here! Here! No visitors allowed on this yere dock without a permission.

CAPTAIN JINKS. I say, Charlie—Gussie—who's got the permission? [*Each one begins with his right-hand pocket, and all look through all their pockets in unison without success; then* Captain JINKS *removes his hat and triumphantly takes out a piece of paper.*] Here you are, Mr. Policeman!

THE POLICEMAN [*not taking the paper*]. All right! [*And passes on.*]

CAPTAIN JINKS [*to* PETER, *who sits whistling on the barrel*]. Well, Horace Greeley, any signs of the Opera Queen yet?

PETER. Nope. Where's the band?

CAPTAIN JINKS. The band has struck, so we did our best without it.

PETER. Well, say, she ain't up yet—she ain't to leave the boat for a couple of hours yet.

CAPTAIN JINKS. What a sell!   [*The men are much*
GUSSIE. What a bore!   *disappointed, and*
CHARLIE. What a damn shame!   *all speak at once.*]

CAPTAIN JINKS

CAPTAIN JINKS. Who told you?

PETER. Jack Tar up there.

At this moment Two Sailors *appear on the ship and struggle down the gang-plank with a large trunk, which they place at one side, and return up the gang-plank.*

CHARLIE. Well, come along, Captain Jinks. We can't hang around here all morning.

GUSSIE. Let's go up town to Union Square and have a drink.

CAPTAIN JINKS. No, no, fellows, we might miss her; some other crowd'll get hold of her and spoil our fun.

CHARLIE. Every one's on the *qui vive* to entertain her. We must fill her time for a week with engagements before she leaves this dock.

GUSSIE. Yes siree, by Jove! so every one in town will see we have the inside track!

CAPTAIN JINKS [*indicating* PETER]. Get rid of the kid.

CHARLIE. Go 'long, Horace Greeley! SCOOT!

PETER. I can't.

CAPTAIN JINKS. Why not?

PETER. I got to sell my papers.

CAPTAIN JINKS. Sell them somewhere else.

CAPTAIN JINKS

PETER. Nope! I got to sell 'em here. If you want me to get out, you got to *buy* me out.

CAPTAIN JINKS. Well, how many papers have you?

PETER. A dollar and a half's worth.

CAPTAIN JINKS. What'll you take for them?

PETER. A dollar sixty!

CAPTAIN JINKS. No, you won't. Come along, boys, chip in fifty cents each. [*He starts singing "Up in a Balloon, Boys." The others join in, diving into their waistcoat pockets, and each pitches half a dollar into* Captain JINKS' *hat.*]

Two Sailors *bring down another big trunk and, depositing it near the first, return to the ship.*

CAPTAIN JINKS [*to* PETER]. Here you are! [*Giving the money.*]

The men stop whistling. The Newsboy *with his cap on one side swaggers off whistling "Up in a Balloon, Boys," but steals immediately back and hides under the gang-plank.*

CAPTAIN JINKS. I say, I'll match you both to see who pays for the landau to take her away.

CHARLIE. In the name of all three of us?

CAPTAIN JINKS. Oh, yes; but match who pays! [*Each gets out his coin.*] You first, Charlie, match me! [*They throw the coins.*]

CAPTAIN JINKS

CHARLIE. Heads!

CAPTAIN JINKS. Good! Gussie! [*He and* GUSSIE *throw.*]

GUSSIE. Tails!

CAPTAIN JINKS. Bravo! You pay for the landau, Gussie. Thank you, old man. [*Shaking his hand.*]

CHARLIE [*also shaking his hand*]. Thank you!

GUSSIE. Botheration!

The Sailors *bring down another trunk.*

CAPTAIN JINKS. Hello, Jack! Is that little Italian bird on board awake yet?

A SAILOR. Oh, yes; she's busy giving presents to all the deck-hands. [*They go back on to the ship.*]

CAPTAIN JINKS. I'll tell you what I'll do, fellows. I'll bet you five hundred dollars— [*Interrupted.*]

CHARLIE. I have n't got it!

CAPTAIN JINKS [*laughing*]. Well, Gussie'll lend it to you, won't you, Gussie?

CHARLIE. That's so. 'Course he will!

CAPTAIN JINKS. I'll bet you both five hundred that I'll make love to her.

CHARLIE [*laughing*]. That's nothing. I'd make love to anything for five hundred dollars.

CAPTAIN JINKS [*laughing*]. Go West! I mean

SKETCH BY PERCY ANDERSON
for *Madame Trentoni*

CAPTAIN JINKS

I'll bet you five hundred dollars I'll get up a flirtation with her.

CHARLIE. Make it a thousand.

CAPTAIN JINKS. Will you lend Charlie a thousand, Gussie?

CHARLIE. Yes; of course he will!

CAPTAIN JINKS. All right. Good!

CHARLIE. Done! [*They shake hands.*] I think I ought to stand some chance with the fair lady— she may have broken the hearts of the blue bloods of Europe, but after all, my great-great-grandfather settled in Maryland, driven from France by the Huguenot troubles, and my family is connected with the royal blood of France. We haven't a cent left, still I think I can hold my own.

CAPTAIN JINKS [*bored*]. Oh, all right, Charlie.

GUSSIE. You're not the only lardy-dah here. My ancestor, the first Van Vorkenburg, came over with Peter Stuyvesant, and was an early Dutch Governor of New York. My family has always been mixed up with the government of the country. My father is a politician now, and so we've never had to work for our living.

CHARLIE. Give us a rest!

CAPTAIN JINKS. Hold on a minute. What's the matter with my family! I'm Captain Jinks of the

CAPTAIN JINKS

Horse Marines, formerly of Richmond, Virginia; a member of one of those real old Southern families you read about, ruined by the Civil War—only, as a matter of fact, we were dead broke before the war began! However, never mind! Now, you boys go and get the landau.

CHARLIE. Not if we know it. She might come out while we were gone and that would give you an advantage. I'm not losing Gussie's thousand so easily! I intend to get up a flirtation with her myself.

GUSSIE. Well, so do I, by Jove!

CAPTAIN JINKS. Oh, do you! Another five hundred that neither of you get your arm around her waist! [*Shaking hands with both quickly.*] And come on now, *we'll all three go* after the landau.

They link arms and go out singing "Walking down Broadway." As they go the Newsboy *climbs up from under the gang-plank and placing two fingers of his hand in his mouth whistles a piercing signal twice— then waves his cap. The* Times Reporter *runs in.*

THE TIMES REPORTER. Is she coming?

PETER. No; but I got sumthin' to tell you—I mean, to *sell* you!

The Policeman *enters and gives the* Sailor *a bit of chewing-tobacco, which he takes and says "Thank ye" for.*

CAPTAIN JINKS

The Times Reporter. What is it?

Peter. Pst! [*Motioning toward the* Sailor *and* Policeman, *who will hear.*]

The Sailor [*who stands by*]. Hello, she's a comin' now, I guess. The old party's between decks with full sail on.

Peter. What do you say to this? [*Motioning the* Times Reporter *to one side, where he whispers to him in dumb show all about the three men and their bet. Surprise, curiosity, and delight are shown by the* Times Reporter. *Meanwhile an official, a* Private Detective, *in plain clothes, has sauntered in and meets the* Policeman, *who has started back toward the street.*]

The Detective [*in semi-confidential tone*]. I understand there's a Oppry Singer on board this here boat who's goin' to land this A. M. with costumes and jewelry and a cart-load of stuff. Not off yet, eh?

The Policeman [*very supercilious*]. Naw!

The Detective. Well, there's a suspicion she may try to do a bit of smuggling, and I'm detailed special to see there's no bribing of our officials. I shall do the examination myself. [*He opens his coat, showing the official badge on his breast.*] Just be on hand in case there's a little job for you.

The Policeman [*with a very different manner—most obsequious—touches his hat*]. Yes, surr.

CAPTAIN JINKS

THE DETECTIVE. Be in ear-shot, and if you hear me whistle twice like this [*whistling twice*]—why, come along.

THE POLICEMAN [*touching his hat*]. Yes, surr. [*He offers the Detective a piece of chewing-tobacco.*]

THE DETECTIVE. Oh, thank you. [*Takes a bite, and returns the "plug."*]

The Policeman *passes out. Meanwhile the* Newsboy *and the* Times Reporter *have finished.*

THE TIMES REPORTER. Look here. Keep mum about this, and I'll make it worth your while. I've got to consult with Mr. Mapleson before I publish a thing like that, but if it ever *is* published, it's got to be *my* story! Why, I ought to get a rise of salary if I get that for my paper.

The Detective *starts to go as four men enter hurriedly, breathless, running in, all with dripping umbrellas,—the* Herald Reporter, *the* Sun Reporter, *the* Tribune Reporter, *and the* Clipper Representative.

ALL THE REPORTERS. Off yet? [*Almost knocking over the* Detective.]

THE DETECTIVE. Excuse me, gentlemen [*and exits*].

THE TIMES REPORTER. No—but she's expected shortly. Where's the Express? the World?

THE CLIPPER REPRESENTATIVE. They're waiting

CAPTAIN JINKS

at the Brevoort House with her maid and old Belliarti.

THE TRIBUNE REPORTER. Where's the bouquet?

THE SUN REPORTER. Here.

They all gather around him and unwrap a huge and beautiful bouquet, which is covered with five different newspapers—the latter soaking wet from the rain.

THE TRIBUNE REPORTER. We protected it from the rain with a representative sheet of each one of us, so as to show no partiality, and have the bouquet represent in every way the United Press of New York!

The bouquet is in the shape of a cone whose base is nearly a yard in diameter. There are two tiers of red and white roses, alternating, and the structure is crowned by one important calla lily. A large bow with streamers of red, white, and blue ribbon adds a last gala and patriotic note!

MRS. GREENBOROUGH *appears on the ship and hesitates at the top of the gang-plank.*

PETER [*aside to the* Sailor]. Come on, let's sell 'em. Here's the old lady—let's pretend she's the Primy Donny!

THE SAILOR [*chuckling*]. You're a rum un! [*He goes up the gang-plank to help* Mrs. GREENBOROUGH.]

CAPTAIN JINKS

PETER. Hi! Pst! [*Whistles again between his fingers; the* Reporters *all turn; the bouquet is unwrapped.*] Here she is!

Mrs. GREENBOROUGH *comes down the gang-plank. She is a pretty, middle-aged lady, kind, motherly, and a little foolish. She has one especial characteristic: she talks whenever starting in a steady stream, but never finishes a speech, as no one will wait for her, but either interrupts or leaves her. When interrupted she invariably stops short with a broad and sweet smile, good-naturedly accepting what has become for her the inevitable. She is dressed a few years behind the times, but is somewhat prejudiced against the quiet colors. All the* Reporters *drop their umbrellas and rush to meet her. They reach the foot of the gang-plank just as she does, and gathering all to the right side, bow low and offer her the big bouquet.*

THE TIMES REPORTER. Welcome, madame, to our great Country! The American Eagle, whose own high C carries from the shores of the Atlantic to the Pacific's golden strand, welcomes her Sister Song-bird! And the Press of New York offer their united compliments and felicitations with the accompanying bouquet. [*Giving the bouquet with a bow which he has copied from one of Lester Wallack's. All the* Reporters *applaud.*]

THE HERALD REPORTER. Bravo, Pat!

CAPTAIN JINKS

The Newsboy *on his barrel and the* Sailor *at the top of the gang-plank are very much amused.* Mrs. Greenborough *is tremendously surprised, and taking the bouquet is followed to one side by all the* Reporters, *who encircle her.*

Mrs. Greenborough. My word! I never was so surprised in all my life, nor so overpowered, nor so fluctuated either, for I'm sure I'm speechless, I can't say a word! Only fancy, this is the first booky I've had donated to me since my old gentleman used to call me pretty pet names in the gone-by days! [*She continues talking a steady stream, but the* Times *and the* Herald Reporters *come away from the others, and speak to each other aside.*]

The Herald Reporter. For Heaven's sake, there must be some mistake.

The Times Reporter. *She* eighteen years old? She's three times eighteen!

The Herald Reporter. Does Mapleson want to tell us the Prince gave *grandma* an emerald bracelet?

Peter [*innocently*]. Gee! I made a mistake. That ain't the party; that must be her mother.

The Times Reporter. Oh, it's the companion, of course! What idiots! Get back the bouquet!

The Herald Reporter. How? [*Calls.*] Bill!

The Tribune Reporter *joins them.*

CAPTAIN JINKS

THE TRIBUNE REPORTER. She can't be— [*Interrupted by*]

THE HERALD REPORTER. No, no, it's the chaperon— Go on—get back the bouquet.

THE TRIBUNE REPORTER. What! get it back? I can't. Here! Pete!

The Sun Reporter *leaves* Mrs. GREENBOROUGH *gladly.*

THE SUN REPORTER. Say, shorthand isn't quick enough to take down *her* conversation.

THE TRIBUNE REPORTER. Don't bother. It's the wrong party. Get back the bouquet.

THE SUN REPORTER. Ask for it, or grab it?

The Clipper Representative *quickly joins them from* Mrs. GREENBOROUGH, *who is still talking and raises her voice a little as they leave her, but seeing their backs toward her breaks off in the middle of a sentence, smiling, and smells her bouquet.*

THE SUN REPORTER, THE TIMES REPORTER, THE TRIBUNE REPORTER, and THE HERALD REPORTER. [*All together.*] We've made a mistake!

The Newsboy *whistles shrilly through his fingers to attract their attention, and they all turn quickly to look as* AURELIA *appears on the ship. She is quite the most lovely creature that ever came, like Venus Aphrodite, from the sea! Youth and beauty join in*

CAPTAIN JINKS

making her adorable, and a charming individuality, with a sense of humor bewilderingly attractive, makes her victory over mere man, irrespective of age or station, child's play. Her modish bustle only accentuates the grace of her girlish figure. And even a "waterfall" only seems to make a friendly background for her perfect brow and finely poised head. She carries in her arms a very small black-and-tan dog; she wears an ermine fur tippet and carries a muff. The Reporters *quickly draw up to one side.* AURELIA *stops at the top of the gang-plank for a moment, looking around her and smiling, and then runs gaily down.*

AURELIA. Hip! hip! hurrah! Here we are at last on American soil—planks—never mind, *soil*—E Pluribus Unum! [*She stands by the foot of the gang-plank. All the* Reporters *raise their hats.*]

MRS. GREENBOROUGH [*accustomed to* AURELIA'S *beauty and at present entirely self-absorbed*]. Oh, Aurelia darling, do look at the beautiful booky these dear Americans have given me; did you ever see— [*Interrupted.*]

AURELIA. No, I never did! Good morning, gentlemen! [*All the* Reporters *bow low.*]

THE TIMES REPORTER [*stepping slightly forward*]. Welcome, madame, to our great Country! The American Eagle, whose own high C carries from the shores of the Atlantic to the Pacific's golden strand,

CAPTAIN JINKS

welcomes her Sister Song-bird! And the Press of New York offer their united compliments and felicitations with the—with—with the bouquet which will arrive at your hotel this evening!

AURELIA. Thank you very much, I'm sure. Here, Mrs. Gee; please hold Camille. [*Giving the small black-and-tan dog to* Mrs. GREENBOROUGH.] I call him "*Camille*" because "*Marguerite Gautier*" is so long, and I wanted to name him after my first great success. You are all the Reporters, aren't you? [*Smiling ravishingly straight into every one of their faces.*] They told me you'd be here. [*She shakes hands all around with each one of them, as she speaks.*] I'm so glad; I'm dying to be interviewed! [*Laughing.*]

THE HERALD REPORTER [*apropos of her walk*]. We see you have the Saratoga stride in England.

AURELIA. You mean my walk? With the Grecian bend? Oh, but we call it the Brighton Dip. Yes, it's very fashionable with us!

THE TRIBUNE REPORTER. To what hotel do you go?

AURELIA. The Brevoort House on the Fifth Avenue at Eighth Street; I'm told that is best and not so far up town as the Fifth Avenue Hotel on the Broadway.

THE TIMES REPORTER. And much nearer the New Academy of Music where you are to sing.

CAPTAIN JINKS

AURELIA. Did Mrs. Greenborough present herself?

MRS. GREENBOROUGH. No, I thought I'd better— [*She stops short with a smile, interrupted.*]

AURELIA. Quite right. This is my aunt, gentlemen. [*Elaborate bows.*] Ballet girls and Opera Comique singers are obliged to have a mother you know, but Grand Opera and Shakespeare can travel with an *aunt*.

MRS. GREENBOROUGH. Fancy, I haven't yet half thanked— [*Smiles, interrupted.*]

AURELIA [*interrupting*]. What lovely weather! I've always heard so much of your American climate.

THE TIMES REPORTER. But we call this very bad.

AURELIA. Not to me, I assure you, who sailed from *Liverpool*. I call it almost sunny! Only, dear me, very warm! [*Taking off her furs and placing them on a trunk.*] They told me it was so cold here!

THE HERALD REPORTER. And how do you like America?

AURELIA. Oh, I adore it! It's superb! [*Looking about her at the little dock, and speaking in the stereotyped manner.*] It's so enormous, so great a country! I'm amazed at its size! [*Then coming down to a more natural manner, she laughs.*] Of course

CAPTAIN JINKS

I've not seen very much yet. What town is that across the river over there? Is that Boston?

THE TIMES REPORTER. No, that's Hoboken!

AURELIA. Oh! a suburb, I presume.

THE TIMES REPORTER. Yes, of *Hamburg.*

AURELIA. I hope to see a great deal of your country. I'm mad to go to A. T. Stewart's shop, and to see Saratoga, which I've heard heaps about! and the very first morning I have free from a rehearsal I've promised myself I shall run over to Niagara Falls and back! [*All the* Reporters *are following her with lightning rapidity, looking up now and then, smiling and nodding to her as she talks.*] Mrs. Gee!

MRS. GREENBOROUGH. Yes, my love?

AURELIA. Do go see why they don't bring out the rest of my luggage! [*To the* Reporters.] There are forty-eight boxes.

MRS. GREENBOROUGH. Don't you want— [*Interrupted.*]

AURELIA. Nothing, dear heart, please go. [Mrs. GREENBOROUGH *goes up the gang-plank into the boat.* AURELIA *continues to the* Reporters.] Did you get that? I have *forty-eight boxes.*

THE TIMES REPORTER. That's a good many more even than Parepa-Rosa brought over!

CAPTAIN JINKS

AURELIA. Oh, but she depended entirely on her voice!

THE TRIBUNE REPORTER. What did you make your début in?

AURELIA. "La Traviata"; has it been sung here yet? [*Sitting on one of her trunks.*]

THE TIMES REPORTER. Oh, yes, often, but we understood there was a probability of changing.

AURELIA [*in surprise*]. Changing? Why?

THE TIMES REPORTER. Well—er—there have been several letters written to the Evening Post asking that you make your début in a less risqué opera.

AURELIA. But it's my *great* success!

THE TIMES REPORTER. The Ladies' Anti-French Literature League is leading the movement. There's a great feeling against the *play*. Lots of people won't go to see it.

AURELIA. But how absurd—no one ever understands what an Italian opera is about! O dear, I hope I shall be a success! I'm awfully nervous. Oh, *please* like me! [*The* Reporters *stop scribbling a moment to throw up their hats and shout.*]

ALL THE REPORTERS. We do!

Two Sailors *bring more luggage and go back.*

AURELIA. I'm afraid you'll think me a very foolish young person, I do so want you to like me. You know I'm really an American!

All the Reporters *look up surprised.*

THE HERALD REPORTER. Really?

AURELIA. Yes, my father came from *Trenton, New Jersey.* [*All the* Reporters *drop their heads quickly to their tablets and go on taking notes at a furious rate.*] That's how I get my name—"Trentoni"—don't you see? I'm a *New Jersey* Italian! My real name is Johnson, but of course that wouldn't look at all well on the bills,—"Miss Aurelia Johnson in Semiramide!" I haven't been in America since I was three years old, but really it does all look familiar! At least I wish it did!

THE TRIBUNE REPORTER [*as they all write*]. You were taught singing in Italy?

AURELIA. Yes, my mother sang in the chorus with Titians, and the night I was born she represented a princess at a ball in the second act—so you see I am really of noble birth! I was left an orphan at three, and then my best friend, Signor Belliarti, took care of me like a father and mother both. You know Papa Belliarti?

THE HERALD REPORTER. Yes, we've heard the story. Your ballet master, I believe?

AURELIA. Yes, bless him! He's worn the same

pattern of clothes for fifty years! Would as soon think of changing his affections as altering the cut of his coat. It was through his friendship with Arditi I had my chance with Mapleson in London, where I've sung principally the last two years.

THE TIMES REPORTER. Do you know the Royal Family?

AURELIA. Er—not intimately—that is to say—*personally*—but I know them very well—*by sight!* You see they don't go to the opera since the death of the Prince Consort.

MRS. GREENBOROUGH [*comes back down the gangplank*]. My dear young gentlemen! She's turned the heads— [*Stops with a smile, interrupted.*]

AURELIA [*rising*]. Please get out my pink dolman, this one is so warm.

MRS. GREENBOROUGH. But tell them how the élite— [*Stops with a smile, interrupted, and goes to a large bundle of shawls, which she undoes and takes out the pink dolman.*]

AURELIA. Oh, yes, the Uppertendom have been entrancingly kind to me. But I'll tell you a secret: I want the big *crowd* to love me! I want to outdo Lydia Thompson! I want to win the hearts of the gallery boys!

PETER [*throws his cap up in the air and shouts*]. Hooray!

CAPTAIN JINKS

AURELIA [*seeing him*]. What a nice boy! Mrs. Gee, give him a sixpence! O dear, how much is a sixpence?

THE TRIBUNE REPORTER. Twelve cents.

AURELIA. Then give him a twelve-cent piece; it's one of those little silver things, you know. [Mrs. GREENBOROUGH *does so.*]

Sailors *bring down more luggage and again go back. A* Telegraph Boy *enters with a telegram.*

TELEGRAPH BOY. Madame Trentoni?

ALL THE REPORTERS [*going to the boy*]. Yes! [*They go back in a body to* AURELIA. *The* Times Reporter *gives her the telegram.*]

AURELIA [*opening it*]. A wire! How entrancing!

TELEGRAPH BOY. Somebody sign? [*The* Tribune Reporter *grandiloquently signs and the* Telegraph Boy *leaves.*]

AURELIA. It's from Mapleson; he'll arrive at four! Didn't expect the ship in till to-morrow! Wasn't it superb, our trip! We broke the record for the Atlantic. A good omen for me. Only think, we crossed in *thirteen* days! It takes your breath away!

THE TRIBUNE REPORTER. We'll cross in less than ten days yet!

AURELIA. O dear, I shouldn't like to go so fast as that; it would make me dizzy!

CAPTAIN JINKS

Mrs. Greenborough. Here is your dolman, my dear. I don't know if— [*Interrupted.*]

The Times Reporter *and* Tribune Reporter *both take hold of the dolman.*

Aurelia [*laughing*]. No, wait! Let me see, there must be no partiality. [*She offers her right arm to the* Herald Reporter, *who pulls off that sleeve.*] Thank you! [*She turns to the* Sun Reporter *and offers her left arm. He pulls off the left sleeve.*] Thank you. [*Taking the jacket from the* Sun Reporter *she gives it to the* Clipper Representative.] Will you give that to Mrs. Greenborough, please. [*He does so, and* Mrs. Greenborough *puts it away among the straps.* Aurelia, *turning to the* Tribune Reporter *and* Times Reporter, *who hold the dolman between them.*] Now together, gentlemen, please. [*She turns her back upon them, and they place the dolman on her shoulders; turning quickly again, she curtsies low to all of the* Reporters, *laughingly.*] Thank you all very much! [*All the* Reporters *take off their hats and bow.*]

Sailors *bring out more luggage.*

The Herald Reporter. Are you interested at all in politics?

Aurelia. Oh, yes, I *adore* politics! Don't all women?

The Herald Reporter. We're having a pretty

severe campaign here between Grant and Greeley. I don't suppose you remember the war?

AURELIA. Oh, yes, I do perfectly. Why, I was thirteen years old.

THE TIMES REPORTER. Impossible! Mr. Mapleson says that you are now only eighteen.

AURELIA. Does he! [*She laughs.*] Oh, well, that's only *operatically* I'm eighteen, but *politically* I'm twenty-two! Of course I never approved of but *one* kind of *slaves—men* slaves!

THE HERALD REPORTER. You have [*looking about him*] *five* here! [*More bows.*]

AURELIA. Bravo! Now, you know an Englishman wouldn't have thought of that till to-night, and then he'd have mailed it to me on a post-card.

THE HERALD REPORTER. Who do you favor for President?

AURELIA [*smiling*]. Oh, I don't know. Who do you?

THE HERALD REPORTER. Ah! but that's what we want to get out of you.

AURELIA [*taking him one side and linking her arm confidentially in his*]. Now look here, let's keep this between ourselves. Who does your Journal?

THE HERALD REPORTER [*rather flattered*]. General Grant!

CAPTAIN JINKS

AURELIA. Of course! [*She shakes hands with the* Reporter.] A great general, and I *adore* soldiers.

THE TRIBUNE REPORTER. No stealing a march!

THE HERALD REPORTER. Oh, that's all right! [*He joins the others.*]

AURELIA [*taking the* Tribune Reporter *to one side*]. What's your paper?

THE TRIBUNE REPORTER. The Tribune, founded by the Democratic candidate for President, Horace Greeley.

AURELIA [*aside to the* Tribune Reporter]. He founded a newspaper, did he? Then he's my man, for what would we artists do without the Press! I adore the Press! [*They rejoin the others.*]

Sailors *bring on more luggage.*

A SAILOR. Will you have the live-stock out, too, mam?

AURELIA. Oh, the darlings! Yes, indeed. [*The* Sailors *go back on to the ship.*] My other dogs. [*To* Mrs. GREENBOROUGH.] But that's not all my luggage?

MRS. GREENBOROUGH. Papa Belliarti and your maid took your stage clothes with them to the hotel early this morning.

AURELIA [*cries out*]. Papa Belliarti was *here*, and I didn't see him!

CAPTAIN JINKS

Mrs. Greenborough. You were asleep, and he would n't have you wakened.

Aurelia [*excitedly*]. Dear old darling! When I have n't slept a wink all night. I was so excited knowing I 'd see him this morning. Let 's make haste. I 'm afraid, gentlemen, I must ask you now to excuse me. Oh, but just wait a minute. Mrs. Gee, give me my camel's-hair shawl from the Queen— *from the Queen!* [*Repeating with emphasis lest the* Reporters *should not catch it, and watching them from the corner of her eye to see the effect, she throws off her dolman and takes from* Mrs. Greenborough *the shawl.*] It is easier to wear during the examination. I—er—I presume you are all taking notes of my dress.

The Herald Reporter [*smiling*]. Well, we're doing our best.

Aurelia. Listen; I'll get Mrs. Gee to help you. Mrs. Gee, give me another hat, too; I 'm tired of this one. Give me *the Empress Eugénie.* [*To the* Reporters.] The last bonnet she designed before her flight from the Tuileries! And it still holds its own. [Mrs. Greenborough *brings it and* Aurelia *puts it on.*]

Mrs. Greenborough. Did you— [*Interrupted.*]

Aurelia. Yes, dear heart; now go with these charming gentlemen and describe all the things

CAPTAIN JINKS

I've worn, *outside* things, (*aside to her*) and just hint at silk linings and Valenciennes lace. I've been told they put everything in their awful papers over here!

MRS. GREENBOROUGH. I'm sure I'll be— [*Interrupted.*]

AURELIA [*pushing her toward the* Reporters]. Of course, who wouldn't be *delighted*, in such alluring company! Good morning, gentlemen!

ALL THE REPORTERS [*bowing*]. Good morning. [*They go off to the street with* Mrs. GREENBOROUGH, *she talking all the time, describing* AURELIA's *dress, etc. The* Herald Reporter *hangs back.*]

AURELIA [*to the* Herald Reporter, *smiling but kindly*]. Don't mind interrupting the dear soul; she expects it, and besides it rests her. We never let her finish a sentence for fear she would die of loss of breath at the end.

THE HERALD REPORTER. Thank you very much. And allow me to promise you a brilliant success. [*He starts to go.*]

AURELIA [*hesitatingly*]. Are *all* Reporters handsome?

THE HERALD REPORTER [*red, but happy*]. They would like to be in *your* eyes, Madame Trentoni. [*He exits in a seventh heaven.*]

CAPTAIN JINKS

AURELIA [*flicking her hand after him, calls*]. Superb! [*She turns to the* Newsboy.] Boy! Come here a minute! Now, between ourselves, tell me something! Which is the best paper here—which do you sell the most?

PETER. Lady, they all was second-class what was here; the only *real* paper in New York is "The Fireside Companion." [Captain JINKS, CHARLIE, *and* GUSSIE *are heard whistling "Captain Jinks" in the distance.*] Ma'am—there's some dandies here now to welcome you; hear 'em! There's been a political parade to-day and they're all togged out in their uniforms! And I tell yer, they're high steppers! A one-ers—blue-blooders, regular lardy-dahs!

The whistling changes to singing, and the three enter from the street singing "Captain Jinks." They stop short in the middle of a word, as they see AURELIA, *who, pretending not to notice them, looks at a label on a trunk. The* Newsboy *whistles* "*Up in a Balloon, Boys,*" *and goes behind a trunk.*

CAPTAIN JINKS. She's off!

GUSSIE. She's a bouquet!

CHARLIE. She's a whole floral emblem! I will certainly do a little flirting here myself! Everything square now, fellows, and the best man wins! Go along, Captain Jinks, introduce your pals.

CAPTAIN JINKS

They step toward AURELIA, *Captain* JINKS *slightly ahead. The* Newsboy *stops whistling.*

CAPTAIN JINKS. I beg your pardon, Madame Trentoni?

AURELIA [*turns*]. Yes?

CAPTAIN JINKS. Pray allow us to welcome you to New York. Your coming turns October into June, and we will not miss the birds this winter, since you will be singing in the Academy trees. [*Offering his bouquet.*]

AURELIA [*takes his bouquet*]. Thank you very much, but remember there are birds—and—*birds!*

CAPTAIN JINKS. May I present Mr. Charles La Martine?

CHARLIE [*bows and gives his bouquet*]. Twice welcome, madam!

CAPTAIN JINKS. And may I present Mr. Augustus Van Vorkenburg? Familiarly known as "Gussie," also "Mother's Darling."

GUSSIE [*to* Captain JINKS]. Shut up! [*Bows and gives his bouquet.*] *Thrice* welcome!

AURELIA. Thank you. [*To* Captain JINKS.] And now won't one of your friends present *you?*

CHARLIE. This is Captain Jinks of the Horse Marines!

CAPTAIN JINKS

AURELIA [*laughing*]. Oh, yes; I've heard of him.

CAPTAIN JINKS [*embarrassed*]. No, no—I am Robert Jinks, tremendously at your service.

AURELIA. It doesn't really make any difference because I never remember names, but you are all very kind. I fancy you are some more reporters.

GUSSIE [*offended*]. Oh, I say, no!

AURELIA [*insinuatingly*]. I thought you might be, they seem to be such *handsome* men!

CHARLIE. No.—

CAPTAIN JINKS. No.—

AURELIA. Oh, then you must be the *editors!*

CAPTAIN JINKS [*laughing*]. No, no, madam, we won't deceive you. We are only three good-for-nothings who have engaged seats in the front row for your entire season.

AURELIA. If you want me to believe that, do put on your hats, for you don't look the parts at all!

CHARLIE. We want to know if there is anything in the world we could do for you?

GUSSIE. We would like to plan something for your amusement; would you tell us your hotel?

AURELIA [*after a second's pause*]. The Fifth Avenue. [GUSSIE, *who is really an ass, ties a knot in his handkerchief so as to remember it.*]

CAPTAIN JINKS

CAPTAIN JINKS. There is to be a croquet match day after to-morrow at the fashionable club, perhaps you would care to go; if so, we would be glad to arrange.

Mrs. GREENBOROUGH *comes back from her walk, having evidently been "shaken" by the* Reporters *at an "early stage in the game."*

AURELIA. You're very kind. I never could understand the game, but my chaperon adores it and would love to come, I'm sure.

CAPTAIN JINKS [*who has not seen* Mrs. GREENBOROUGH]. We should be charmed.

GUSSIE. It'll be very dressy!

AURELIA. Dear Mrs. Gee, I want to present to you three New York *gentlemen* who have most kindly come to welcome us — Mrs. Greenborough.

The three men bow, saying, "Madam," but with a note of poignant disappointment in their voices.

AURELIA. And they *want* you, dear, to go to a croquet match with them.

MRS. GREENBOROUGH [*overjoyed*]. My word, and that will be a treat! Thank you very much, gentlemen! My love, here come your pets, what shall — [*Interrupted, as the* Sailors *enter with two large dogs — a Newfoundland and a white Spitz — and a very large cage containing a small live monkey. The*

CAPTAIN JINKS

Second Sailor *returns to the boat, after putting the monkey down beside the gang-plank.*]

AURELIA. Oh, yes, the darlings. [*Going to meet the* Sailor *with the dogs. She stops to speak to* Mrs. GREENBOROUGH.] Did you tell the reporters about that beastly monkey?

MRS. GREENBOROUGH. Oh, no, I forgot.

AURELIA. My dear, how careless of you! So long as Mapleson insists on my having the horrid thing, you should have said the Khedive of Egypt gave him to me; that would have sounded superbly. [*She goes to the* Sailor *and takes the leaders of the two dogs from him; the* Sailor *goes back on to the boat.*] You blessed old dogs, you! The poor things must be mad for a little exercise. Oh! Mr.——? [*In front of* CHARLIE.]

CHARLIE [*flattered at being especially addressed*]. La Martine. [*Bowing.*]

AURELIA. You said you wanted to do something for me; will you take Leonora for a walk?

CHARLIE. I beg your pardon?

AURELIA [*giving him the leader of the Newfoundland dog*]. This is Leonora, out of "Trovatore," you know. Just a bit of a stroll and back, say ten minutes? [*Looking him straight in the eyes and smiling sweetly.*]

CAPTAIN JINKS

CHARLIE. With pleasure, if I must n't go alone?

AURELIA. Certainly not. [*She crosses to* GUSSIE.] Mr. Dundreary—

GUSSIE [*bowing*]. Augustus Bleeker van Vorkenburg.

AURELIA. What a *grand* name! You 'll go along and take Rosina—"Barber of Seville"—*won't* you —"*Gussie*"?—

GUSSIE. Ah! but Charlie and I are no company for each other.

AURELIA [*gaily*]. I see! You want ladies' society. Mrs. Gee! Mrs. Gee! [*Taking her arm.*] You want a little walk, too. Yes, you do! You 'll never get that extra ten pounds off if you lose a single morning. Take *Camille* along! [*Giving her the black-and-tan.*] Now be off. Good-by, *darlings; that's* for the *dogs!*

CHARLIE [*turning*]. Which pair?

AURELIA [*laughing*]. Clever! very clever!

CHARLIE, GUSSIE, *and the three dogs and* Mrs. GREENBOROUGH *exit*, Mrs. GREENBOROUGH *talking about how glad she is for a glimpse of land.*

CAPTAIN JINKS. Have you saved the monkey for me?

AURELIA. Oh! I wish you would! *Will you? Take* him and lose him. I 'm afraid of him, you know.

CAPTAIN JINKS

CAPTAIN JINKS. Then why do you keep him?

AURELIA. It's Mapleson's idea. He thinks it makes me interesting. Though why a monkey should do that, I don't know, and I'd sleep happier to-night if that wretched animal was out of the way.

CAPTAIN JINKS. Would you mind walking a few steps over in that direction and keeping your back turned?

AURELIA. What are you going to do? [*She goes a few steps to the left and stands with her back turned.*]

Captain JINKS *goes to the* Newsboy, *who is enjoying himself with the monkey in the cage. At the same time the* Sailor *comes out and down the gang-plank and calls to* AURELIA.

THE SAILOR. Miss! Mam!

AURELIA [*with her back turned*]. Do you mean me?

CAPTAIN JINKS. Don't turn, please, till I tell you.

The Policeman *comes slowly along.*

THE SAILOR [*on the gang-plank*]. Don't you want me to get the Inspector for yer, yer things is all out?

AURELIA. Oh, yes, please do. I do want to get away.

THE POLICEMAN. All right, Jack, I 'm passin'; I 'll send him along.

CAPTAIN JINKS

THE SAILOR. Thank'y. [*Exits on boat.* Policeman *walks on.*]

PETER [*who has been told by* Captain JINKS *he may have the monkey for his own if he will take it away, jumps up with a wild howl of delight*]. Hiyi! to keep!

CAPTAIN JINKS. Shh! Yes. [*Whispering.*] Hurry now, and quiet. [*Motioning him off with the cage— the* Newsboy *seizes it.*]

AURELIA. May I turn now?

CAPTAIN JINKS. In two minutes.

The Newsboy, *rushing past the* Policeman *with the cage, is at this moment nabbed by him.*

THE POLICEMAN. Here! Where are you going with that animal?

CAPTAIN JINKS. That's all right—it's my affair—have a drink? [*Gives him a quarter. The* Newsboy *passes out with monkey.*]

THE POLICEMAN. Thank ye, sir, you're a gentleman, sir. [*Goes.*]

CAPTAIN JINKS [*to* AURELIA]. Now! The monkey's gone, and you saw nothing, know nothing, so you see you can't be blamed. Mapleson can complain in the papers and have the docks better policed.

AURELIA. Really, you've made yourself my friend for life!

CAPTAIN JINKS

CAPTAIN JINKS. I hope to be permitted to take the monkey's place, so far as being often in your company is concerned.

AURELIA. Don't you think you young men were rather impertinent, however?

CAPTAIN JINKS. Yes, now I've met you I think we were. Still, I hope you'll forgive us.

AURELIA. Oh, I will, *you*.—

CAPTAIN JINKS. And I hope I'll deserve that. Please, isn't there anything I could do for you? I don't suppose you know many people here.

AURELIA. Not a soul.

CAPTAIN JINKS. And you must go about—there's lots to see. Please let me take you. I'm more or less of an idiot, I know, but so are most men— [*Interrupted.*]

AURELIA. Yes, it's not much of a distinction.

CAPTAIN JINKS. I was going to add so far as *women* are concerned!

AURELIA. Oh! I beg your pardon.

CAPTAIN JINKS. Really, joking aside, I ask you—mayn't I call upon you at your hotel?

AURELIA. I'll think it over.

CAPTAIN JINKS. To-day?

AURELIA. No, I shall spend to-day with my dear

CAPTAIN JINKS

foster-father. You know Professor Belliarti? He came over a month ago to drill the ballet. The first time we've been separated since I was three years old! [*She has forgotten herself and is speaking with real feeling.*] He's the sweetest, dearest, most unselfish old creature, who has given me everything I have in the world— [*She stops short, suddenly realizing what she is saying.*] Oh, I beg your pardon for going on so!

CAPTAIN JINKS [*sympathetically*]. You needn't beg my pardon, for I can match your old gentleman with a dear little old lady living on a plantation far away down in Virginia, who's done her very *darndest* for me.

They look at each other a moment without speaking, with a mutual understanding of each other's nature.

AURELIA. You *may* come and see me—to-morrow. [*She gives him her hand.*]

CAPTAIN JINKS [*taking her hand*]. Thank you.

Mrs. STONINGTON *and* Miss MERRIAM *come timidly from the street. They are of middle age, and dressed a trifle out of date. Miss* MERRIAM, *who is of a decidedly shrinking nature, is attired in a vivid shade of "bottle green" heavily laid upon black. A quantity of green fringe, however, hints at her heart being still young and her spirits capable of gaiety, a fact also abetted by a spotted net over her "water-*

CAPTAIN JINKS

fall." Mrs. STONINGTON, *more dominant, and evidently the spokeswoman, favors a strict magenta in her apparel. Both are simple, good-hearted, kindly intentioned, but misguided ladies, the Vice-President and Secretary of the Anti-French Literature League; they act quite without malice.* Miss MERRIAM *is deaf and dumb.*

MRS. STONINGTON. I beg pardon; can you tell me where to find Madame Trentoni?

AURELIA. *I* am Madame Trentoni.

MRS. STONINGTON. Oh, really! [*She turns and with her fingers tells* Miss MERRIAM *that this is* Madame TRENTONI. *She then introduces her companion.*] This is Miss Merriam, the Corresponding Secretary. [Miss MERRIAM *bows smilingly.*]

AURELIA. How do you do?

MRS. STONINGTON. And *I* am Mrs. Stonington, the Vice-President of the Anti-French Literature League.

AURELIA. How do you do. [*Aside to* Captain JINKS.] I thought they had come to apply for places in the ballet!

While AURELIA *is speaking to* Captain JINKS, Miss MERRIAM *has talked on her fingers to* Mrs. STONINGTON. AURELIA *turns before she finishes and shows her surprise at* Miss MERRIAM's *behavior.*

(44)

CAPTAIN JINKS

Mrs. Stonington. My friend says to tell you at once that she is deaf and dumb, but she will be able to understand perfectly what you say from the motion of your lips.

Aurelia [*rather satirically*]. How interesting!

Mrs. Stonington. I presume you have not had much experience in singing to deaf and dumb people—what I mean to say is, that you don't understand the language.

Aurelia. Not at all. Will you sit down? [*Motioning to some trunks.* Mrs. Stonington *and* Miss Merriam *sit.*]

Mrs. Stonington. Thank you. [*She looks up at* Captain Jinks.] Signor Trentoni, I presume? [*Captain* Jinks *bows in elaborate acquiescence.*]

Aurelia [*laughing in spite of herself*]. No, no! How dare you! This is—a *friend* of mine who has kindly come to welcome me.

Captain Jinks. Mr. Jinks. [*Bowing. The two ladies bow back.*]

Mrs. Stonington [*to* Captain Jinks]. *Do* sit. [*He does so on another trunk. He and* Aurelia *are much amused.* Miss Merriam *nods her head and smiles acquiescence during all of* Mrs. Stonington's *speeches.*] We read in the papers this morning you had arrived sooner than expected, and we decided to come right down and take the bull by the horns.

AURELIA. Meaning *me*, I presume? [*Trying hard not to laugh.*]

MRS. STONINGTON. Er—yes— [*She is interrupted by* Miss MERRIAM, *who tugs at her arm and makes a few rapid movements with her fingers.*]

MRS. STONINGTON. Yes, dear, and just like you! [*To* AURELIA.] She's so sensitive! She thinks it would be politer to say take the cow by the horns.

AURELIA. What can I do for you?

MRS. STONINGTON. It is stated in the papers that you intend to make your debutt in a piece called Traviatter, which I am given to understand by a number of the members of our League who have read the book is the French drammer "La Dame aux Camélias."

AURELIA. The papers and the League members are quite right.

MRS. STONINGTON. I am told the heroine is a— young person—no better than she should be, in fact not so good.

Miss MERRIAM *tugs violently at* Mrs. STONINGTON'S *arm and makes a few rapid passes with her fingers.*

MRS. STONINGTON. Of course! I never thought.

CAPTAIN JINKS

[*To* AURELIA.] Excuse me, but would your gentleman friend be so kind as to walk to the other end of the dock for a few minutes?

AURELIA. Certainly. My friend is a very gallant man, Mrs. Vice-President; I am sure he would jump off the dock, if a lady asked him.

CAPTAIN JINKS. Not by a long shot!

MRS. STONINGTON [*seriously*]. But I shouldn't think of asking such a thing; he might get drowned.

CAPTAIN JINKS [*rising*]. Shall I go?

AURELIA. Yes, please, just for a second or two.

Captain JINKS *withdraws outside by the boat.*

MRS. STONINGTON. Our mission is a very delicate one.

AURELIA. I think I should call it indelicate—

MRS. STONINGTON. Oh, no! we want to ask you to make your debutt in some other opera. And we have here a petition to that effect, signed by over six hundred women and school children of Harlem, Brooklyn, and Jersey City—oh, yes, and Williamsburg. [*Handing to* AURELIA *the paper.*]

AURELIA. Thank you so much! What a splendid advertisement!

MRS. STONINGTON. We heard your voice was *most* beautiful, and a *great* many of us want to hear you, who could n't go to *that* opera.

AURELIA. But do you know, when you come right down to the stories of the opera, I don't think there's much choice between them.

MRS. STONINGTON. O dear me, yes! [Miss MERRIAM *nods her head quietly but firmly, and with a sweet smile.*]

AURELIA. Well, what one would you propose?

MRS. STONINGTON [*triumphantly*]. "*Faust!*" [Miss MERRIAM *looks transported as she recalls the angels of the final scene.*]

AURELIA. Oh, but that is n't a goody-goody story by any means!

MRS. STONINGTON. My dear! it's a *sweet* opera! I remember the beautiful tableau, like the death of little Eva, at the end.

AURELIA. I suppose you did n't notice that Mephistopheles seems to have got Marguerite after all; for the angels always take up quite a different young lady—and seem perfectly unconscious of their mistake.

MRS. STONINGTON. Never mind, the story is so pure.

AURELIA. But do you know what happens between the second and third acts?

MRS. STONINGTON. On the stage?

CAPTAIN JINKS

AURELIA. O dear, no! in the story.

MRS. STONINGTON. Faust and Marguerite get married.

AURELIA. No, they don't; that's the trouble.

MRS. STONINGTON [*staggered*]. *What!!!*

AURELIA. They *didn't!*

MRS. STONINGTON. Bless my soul! [*She rises aghast.* Miss MERRIAM *pulls* Mrs. STONINGTON's *arm and makes a few rapid signs.*]

MRS. STONINGTON [*to* Miss MERRIAM]. *I should say so!* [*Kisses her gratefully.*] [*To* AURELIA.] She says she's glad we asked that young man to go away.

Miss MERRIAM *again pulls* Mrs. STONINGTON's *elbow and motions.*

MRS. STONINGTON. You dear thing, how like you! [*To* AURELIA.] She wants to know why you don't make your debutt in Oratorier. Come along now, do! [Miss MERRIAM *tugs again at* Mrs. STONINGTON's *arm, and makes a few more finger movements.*] Yes! [*To* AURELIA.] The women of America ask you to sing in Oratorier!

Captain JINKS *is heard whistling* "Champagne Charlie is My Name."

AURELIA [*who can hardly restrain her laughter*]. I'll tell you what I'll do, I'm willing if you can persuade my manager; you see, really, these things are entirely in the hands of Mr. Mapleson.

MRS. STONINGTON. We'll see him at once.

Miss MERRIAM *tugs* Mrs. STONINGTON's *elbow and motions.*

MRS. STONINGTON. Quite so! [*To* AURELIA.] She says men are so *easy*, we shall consider it settled!

CAPTAIN JINKS [*stops whistling to call*]. I'm whistling so as not to hear. Must I take another trip?

AURELIA. No, come in!

Captain JINKS *returns.*

AURELIA [*to* Mrs. STONINGTON]. Mr. Mapleson arrives this afternoon from Boston and will stop at the New York Hotel.

MRS. STONINGTON. Thank you. If you should need some extra ladies in the chorus for the Oratorier, I would come,— I know most of them, having belonged to the Oratorier Society for many years. We wear white dresses with blue sashes across the left shoulder, which makes a very pretty effect. [Miss MERRIAM *tugs* Mrs. STONINGTON's *arm and makes a few motions.* Mrs. STONINGTON *nods her head and turns to* AURELIA.] And Miss Merriam always goes with me; she fills up and makes the chorus look bigger.

AURELIA. All of that, of course, will be left with Mr. Mapleson.

CAPTAIN JINKS

CAPTAIN JINKS [*with difficulty restraining his laughter*]. Do they have men singers in an Oratorio?

MRS. STONINGTON. O dear me, yes, we have some very handsome gentlemen singers in the club!

CAPTAIN JINKS. I wish you'd just mention me to Mr. Mapleson as a candidate.

MRS. STONINGTON [*smiling apologetically*]. I'm afraid I couldn't do that. Don't you think it would look rather bold my suggesting a young man and a perfect stranger? [Miss MERRIAM *tugs* Mrs. STONINGTON'S *elbow and makes a few motions.*] Yes. [*To* AURELIA.] We won't keep you any longer; we're very much obliged to you I'm sure, and the League will signify their gratefulness by giving you an afternoon reception in the rooms of the Young Men's Christian Association. Good-by. [*Bows.*]

Miss MERRIAM *also smiles and bows.*

AURELIA [*also bowing*]. Good-by.

Mrs. STONINGTON *takes* Miss MERRIAM'S *arm and they turn their backs to* AURELIA *a second to consult.* Mrs. STONINGTON *motions a moment.* Miss MERRIAM *nods her head delightedly. They both turn and go to* AURELIA *with outstretched hands, very pleased with themselves for the gracious thing they think they are doing.*

MRS. STONINGTON. Good-by. [*She and* AURELIA

shake hands. AURELIA *says good-by; then* Miss MERRIAM *and* AURELIA *shake hands and* AURELIA *again says good-by.*]

MRS. STONINGTON [*to explain and excuse their cordiality*]. She says we don't consider *singers actresses.*

AURELIA. Very few are!

Mrs. STONINGTON *and* Miss MERRIAM *leave the dock in a manner of pleased satisfaction.*

AURELIA [*laughingly to* Captain JINKS]. What do you think Mapleson will do with them?

CAPTAIN JINKS [*laughing*]. "Men are so easy!"

AURELIA. Ah, but she, poor thing, was deaf and dumb! the only kind of woman who ever would have said that.

CAPTAIN JINKS. I should hate a silent woman in a house. It would be like a bird who could n't sing, a rose that had no scent, a baby that could n't cry, a piano never played upon.

AURELIA. Oh, I don't suppose there ever was a piano that did n't at least once do its worst with Rubenstein's Melody in F! Is this the Inspector! [*As the* Private Detective *enters with the* Policeman. *The* Detective *has a folded paper in his hand.*]

CAPTAIN JINKS. I reckon he is.

The Detective *and* Policeman *pass among the trunks, counting them.*

CAPTAIN JINKS

AURELIA. I'm so nervous about the customs; I wish the whole thing were over. We hear such awful tales at home about them. I haven't a thing dutiable, of course, not a thing! I've only forty-eight boxes anyway, and they contain only my few personal effects!

CAPTAIN JINKS. I'll see what I can do with him to make him lenient as possible.

THE DETECTIVE [*aside to the* Policeman]. Keep in hearing distance of my whistle—if they're going to try any bribing tricks it'll be soon now. [*The* Policeman *passes on and the* Detective *approaches* AURELIA.] Madam Trentoni?

AURELIA. Yes, sir. I hope you're not going to disturb everything; the boxes were so *beautifully* packed!

THE DETECTIVE. I must do my duty, madam.

CAPTAIN JINKS. We expect you to do that, officer, only don't exaggerate it!

THE DETECTIVE. Your husband, madam?

CAPTAIN JINKS. That's not your business!

AURELIA [*to* Captain JINKS]. Oh, don't make him angry! [*To the* Detective, *very sweetly, but with some nervousness.*] It's a friend who came down to meet me. I had a splendid crossing! Do you like ocean travelling?

CAPTAIN JINKS

THE DETECTIVE. Never tried it. Would you prefer a woman examiner, mam?

AURELIA. Oh, no, I think I'd rather have a man. Unless, of course, you're going to be personal! If you're going to look for violins in the flounces of my petticoats, and diamonds in my bustle, I'd rather have a *lady*—a *perfect* lady!

THE DETECTIVE [*looking at her*]. I don't consider there'll be any need for that.

AURELIA. There! I knew the minute I saw you, you were going to be sweet and nice and obliging, and I'm going to be equally so, and help you all I can.

CHARLIE *and* GUSSIE *return from their walk with the two dogs, followed by* Mrs. GREENBOROUGH, *who is talking, although a little breathless from having been evidently hurried in her walk. She is interrupted by* AURELIA.

MRS. GREENBOROUGH. My word, though, gentlemen, you do walk fast; it's more—

AURELIA. Come along, Mrs. Gee; we want the keys.

MRS. GREENBOROUGH [*joining her by the trunks*]. Has the— [*Interrupted.*]

AURELIA. Yes, this is the Inspector.

MRS. GREENBOROUGH [*excitedly*]. How do you do,

CAPTAIN JINKS

sir! We haven't a thing, not a single solitary— [*Interrupted.*]

AURELIA. I've told him, Mrs. Gee. [*To the Detective.*] By the bye, you will find a box of new-looking curls and a couple of waterfalls, but they've been worn heaps of times—*by me*, I mean, as well as by the lady who grew 'em!

MRS. GREENBOROUGH [*to* Captain JINKS]. Would you hold Camille?

AURELIA [*smiling to* Captain JINKS *as he takes the dog*]. You see, you are to have your chance after all!

AURELIA *and the* Detective *begin unlocking and arranging the trunks. The* Detective *shows that he is very suspicious of* AURELIA *and of* Captain JINKS. Captain JINKS *joins* CHARLIE *and* GUSSIE *at one side, while* Mrs. GREENBOROUGH *opens the trunks.*

CHARLIE. Well?

CAPTAIN JINKS. Well, what?

CHARLIE. How did you get on?

CAPTAIN JINKS. How do you mean?

CHARLIE. Why, with Trentoni! You've had a tremendous advantage over us!

CAPTAIN JINKS. Oh! Oh, yes, our bet. That's off; she's too good for that sort of thing.

CHARLIE. No you don't! look here, our bet holds

good—a thousand dollars to me if I win, and another thousand if *you don't*.

CAPTAIN JINKS. Nothing of the sort; both bets are off—they were only a joke, and a poor one!

CHARLIE. Here, no sneaking, a bet's a bet!

CAPTAIN JINKS. Not when it's an insult to a lady! And I won't permit any action in regard to Madame Trentoni unworthy of the highest woman in the land.

CHARLIE. Who appointed you her protector? You've bet me one thousand dollars you'd make love to her.

CAPTAIN JINKS. Wait! [*Gives the dog Camille to* GUSSIE.] I haven't quite a thousand with me, but —[*takes card and writes*] I O U $1000 for bet in reference to Madame Trentoni. There you are; you understand? There's no bet about anybody's making love to the lady! *The bet is off!*

AURELIA. Captain Jinks! Will you please help us a moment?

GUSSIE. Here! [*Offering back the dog.*]

CAPTAIN JINKS. No, *you* keep *Camille!* [***He joins*** AURELIA.]

GUSSIE [*to* CHARLIE]. Are you going to let him off?

CHARLIE. No, indeed! He's got to stand by his bet with me, and I intend to win. You must help me, Gussie!

CAPTAIN JINKS

GUSSIE. How, old fellow?

CHARLIE. I've been pumping the old lady on our walk, and she's even a bigger prize than I thought. She's rich as Crœsus and gets a salary for singing that would knock *you* off your feet, Gussie.

GUSSIE. Really! Dear me!

CHARLIE. Yes—Jinks doesn't know, and don't tell him. I'm not only going to win my bet with him, I'm going to *marry her!*

GUSSIE. By Jove! You *are* going it, aren't you?

CHARLIE. You help me, and when I've married the lady, I'll pay you all I owe you.

GUSSIE. Thanks, old fellow. But suppose Captain Jinks—

CHARLIE. He'd never *marry* her; he belongs to two of the most stuck-up families, North or South, in the country! But if he tries to interfere with me in any way, we'll cook his goose for him all the same.

GUSSIE. How? He's such an attractive dog! Don't you think so?

CHARLIE. If he gets on the inside track I'll show him up to her—say he made a bet with us to marry her on account of her money, and show his I O U for proof.

GUSSIE. But he *didn't* bet that.

CAPTAIN JINKS

CHARLIE. What's the odds! You're no Georgie Washington! and you must back me up or lose every cent I owe you.

GUSSIE. I suppose I must n't let myself make a deep impression on her for fear of interfering with *you*.

CHARLIE [*amused*]. Oh, you can try your luck! Come along now. [*They join the others.*] Can we be of any assistance?

AURELIA. Oh, you are—a very great deal with the dogs! I'm really awfully obliged to you. Come along, I'll walk with you to the end of the dock— it's stopped raining, has n't it? [*She turns to go with the two men. The* Detective *has just begun to pitch out the contents of a trunk rather roughly on to the floor.* Mrs. GREENBOROUGH *screams, which stops* AURELIA.]

MRS. GREENBOROUGH. Oh! Aurelia! Look what he's doing!

CAPTAIN JINKS. Say, old man, is that necessary? Go on, hurry up, get through and come out and have a drink with me.

THE DETECTIVE [*looking at* Captain JINKS *very suspiciously*]. No, thank you.

AURELIA. If you ruin my clothes I shall sue the city—I warn you of that! Do you take me for an Irish dressmaker with a French name smuggling in

CAPTAIN JINKS

her winter models! My dear man, go on! Play hide-and-seek in every box if you like! Climb down all the corners, use my hats for tenpins, empty out the shoes, scatter my lingerie to the winds! *Jump on every stitch I own!* And then they call this a *free* country!! Captain Jinks, I leave not my honor, but something much more fragile, I leave my *wardrobe* in your hands! Now, gentlemen. [*And turning she goes out with* CHARLIE *and* GUSSIE.]

MRS. GREENBOROUGH. You old ogre, you!

THE DETECTIVE. I don't take no interest in woman's clothes—I'm just doing my duty. [*He throws open a hat box with three hats in it, and then begins to empty another trunk.* MRS. GREENBOROUGH *is busy trying to repack after him.*]

MRS. GREENBOROUGH. My word! It's a cruel shame! One would think you expected passengers to swim across the Atlantic, like that Lady Godiva, without a stitch on their backs! Another thing, I'm sure it's a great pity, seeing that you're going to display Madame Trentoni's entire wardrobe, we didn't ask those nice young men who gave me a bouquet to stay and take notes for their papers. [*The* Detective *goes to a certain trunk.* Mrs. GREENBOROUGH *sees him and rises, crying out:*] No! No! You mustn't open that; I really do object now!

THE DETECTIVE [*very suspicious*]. Oh, you especially object now! [*His hand is on the lid.*] Kindly give me the key!

MRS. GREENBOROUGH [*sits on the trunk*]. I won't! I appeal to your delicacy as a—as a—*gentleman.* That contains her—her—linen garments and Valenciennes lace.

THE DETECTIVE [*still suspicious*]. Sounds very pretty—I must trouble you for the key.

MRS. GREENBOROUGH [*gives it to him*]. Toad! [*The* Detective *unlocks and opens the trunk.* Professor BELLIARTI *and* MARY, AURELIA's *maid, enter from the street.*] Oh, Professor Belliarti, I'm so pleased you've come back! This dreadful man is making such an exposé of all Aurelia's clothes.

The Policeman *strolls in again.*

PROFESSOR BELLIARTI. That can't be helped, my dear Mrs. Greenborough. Where is Aurelia?

AURELIA [*speaking most joyfully from the outside*]. I hear a voice! I hear a voice I *love!* [*She rushes in and across the stage into* BELLIARTI's *arms, throwing her own about his neck.*]

MARY *has gone to the trunks and is putting them in order. She is joined by the* Policeman, *who helps her lock one of the trunks, the keys being in all the locks. When this is done they stand on one side and talk, both enjoying themselves very much.* MARY *is*

SKETCH BY PERCY ANDERSON
for *Miss Merriam*

pretty and the Policeman *is appreciative. The* Detective *is searching through the trunks.*

PROFESSOR BELLIARTI [*with a voice broken with happy emotion and holding* AURELIA *close in his arms*]. God bless my little girl, God bless my little Taglioni! Glad to see her old crow of a father, eh? Bless your pretty eyes, my Fanny Elssler, my little singing bird!

AURELIA. Oh, Papa Belliarti! Oh, Papa Belliarti! Oh! Oh! Oh! [*Gives him three big hugs.*] I am so glad to see you! [*Half crying, half laughing with joy.*] It was awful disembarking here without a soul to meet me—a soul I loved; for it's home I've come to after all, isn't it? You've always taught me this *was home!* [*Then with a little change of manner.*] I did my best, but I'm afraid I've made dreadful mistakes already, and said the wrong things! But I don't care now I've got you! [*Choking up again.*] I tried to be gay, but to tell the truth I'm so homesick, and all I want is to have a good cry *here* in your arms! [*Breaking down.*]

Captain JINKS *stands watching the* Detective *closely. The* Detective *notices this.* Captain JINKS *gets out his purse and deliberately chooses a few bills and doubles them up, doing it so the* Detective *will see. The* Detective *does see. Only the* Policeman *is blind because he has* MARY *in his eyes.*

CAPTAIN JINKS

PROFESSOR BELLIARTI. That'll be all right now —we have beautiful rooms for you, and they are full of flowers that have been sent, and the rain is over.

AURELIA. And so is mine. [*Wiping her eyes.*] There! See, the sun's out! [*Smiling up at him and holding his hand and linking their arms together.*] It really is you! And you are well! Tell me you are well! Of course you are, and as fat as ever! [BELLIARTI *being slender as a reed.*] You dear old darling you! Come, let me introduce to you these gentlemen who have very courteously come to welcome me. Gentlemen, I want to present to you my best friend and foster-father, Professor Belliarti—a *great artist* in dancing, I can tell you that too.

PROFESSOR BELLIARTI [*with a quaint old-fashioned bow*]. Gentlemen!

CAPTAIN JINKS. Honored sir.

CHARLIE [*at same time, bowing*]. Very pleased.

GUSSIE. Delighted.

AURELIA [*to* BELLIARTI]. And now I want you to see my cabin, how nice it was. Come along into the boat! [*She leads him toward the gang-plank. She sees* MARY *and the* Policeman. AURELIA *exchanges an amused glance with* BELLIARTI.]

AURELIA. Mary! [MARY *does n't hear.*] Mary!!

CAPTAIN JINKS

MARY. Yes, madam? [*She blushes.*]

The Policeman *slides out the big door suddenly.*

AURELIA. I only want to remind you, Mary, you are not in London! And let me warn you—as a *friend*, Mary—that the policemen here are *not English!*

PROFESSOR BELLIARTI. No, they are *Irish*, Mary, so look out for Blarney!

AURELIA. And incidentally, Mary, you had better go on with the packing.

PROFESSOR BELLIARTI [*to the* Detective]. You don't need to keep Madame Trentoni if the maid stays?

THE DETECTIVE. No, sir.

AURELIA. Delightful. Then we can go at once! Come and see my cabin first.

PROFESSOR BELLIARTI. Will one of you gentlemen kindly call a hack?

CAPTAIN JINKS, CHARLIE, and GUSSIE. Oh! please take my *landau! My landau's* at your disposal.

AURELIA [*laughing on the gang-plank*]. But I can't go in the landau of all three!

CAPTAIN JINKS. Oh, yes, you can, it's the *same* landau!

AURELIA. Then I accept with pleasure.

CAPTAIN JINKS

Papa BELLIARTI *disappears on the ship.*

CHARLIE. I'll tell the driver to back in. [*Goes out to the street.*]

GUSSIE *helps* Mrs. GREENBOROUGH *with a trunk-strap.*

AURELIA [*on the gang-plank*]. Oh, Captain Jinks.

CAPTAIN JINKS [*going up to her*]. Yes?

AURELIA. Not to-morrow!

CAPTAIN JINKS [*tremendously disappointed*]. No?

AURELIA. No! This afternoon at four. [*Gives him her hand, which he kisses. She also goes on board and out of sight.*]

CAPTAIN JINKS. This afternoon at four! [*After dreaming a moment, he pulls himself together and beckons to the* Detective.] One minute! [*Motioning him to one side, with him. The* Detective *goes, expecting what is going to happen.*] Look here, now, it's all right—the lady's all right, and you and I are all right. We understand each other, don't we?

THE DETECTIVE. I rather think we do, sir!

CHARLIE *returns.*

CAPTAIN JINKS. Good! rush her things through now and don't bother her any more! [*Giving him the bills.*]

CAPTAIN JINKS

THE DETECTIVE. Thank you. [*Taking them. He blows his whistle twice as agreed on. The* Policeman *quickly enters.*] Officer, I give this man in charge for bribing a United States official.

General consternation.

CAPTAIN JINKS [*dumfounded*]. But—

THE POLICEMAN [*linking his arm in* Captain JINKS']. Come along! Don't make no trouble now! Come along quietly!

The Policeman *exits with* Captain JINKS. GUSSIE *and* CHARLIE *are delighted. The maid is surprised. The* Detective *is satisfied.*

AURELIA [*coming back from the boat*]. Wasn't it charming really? and only think, only thirteen days crossing. [Papa BELLIARTI *follows her.*]

CHARLIE. The landau's ready! [*A large landau backs on from the street.*]

AURELIA. Oh, a superb turnout! Come along, Mrs. Gee! [*And she gets in with* Mrs. GREENBOROUGH *and* BELLIARTI, *the two men helping them, and all talking at once. The bouquets are put in too.*] Really, gentlemen, you've been superbly kind! Really, I shan't forget it—you know, you're very attractive!

GUSSIE. Which one of us is most so?

AURELIA [*leaning out and over the side of the*

carriage]. Impossible to say, you're all so perfectly charming! But where is Captain Jinks?

CHARLIE. Oh, he was called away suddenly, *by most important business!*

AURELIA. Tell him not to forget this afternoon at four!

CHARLIE. This afternoon at four.

PROFESSOR BELLIARTI [*to the driver*]. The Brevoort House. [*The landau starts off.*]

AURELIA. Good-by, good-by!

ALL. Good-by! good-by!

Mrs. GREENBOROUGH *throws back a bouquet, which* CHARLIE *catches, and as the landau passes out of sight, with laughter and good-bys, the curtain falls.*

THE END OF ACT I

THE SECOND ACT

THE SECOND ACT

A FORTNIGHT LATER—Madame TRENTONI's *private parlor in the Brevoort House; a large room with double folding doors at the back which lead into another and larger room. There are two windows on the left side, and a door and mantel on the right. The walls are tinted a light, cold, ugly violet, with a deep crimson velvet paper border. The furniture is gilt and upholstered with crimson satin with heavy red rope worsted fringe. It is comfortable and warm, especially in the summer! and is not plain but hideous. At the windows are lace curtains with heavy satin lambrequins. There is a piano, open, by the windows, in one of which is a very small basket, with a very large handle, full of roses. There is a marble-topped centre-table bearing a Bible, a guide to the city, and a silver-plated card-receiver. An oval-framed steel engraving called "Autumn" (a young lady most inappropriately dressed for that season of the year, with curvature of the spine, and balancing a prize bunch of grapes on the top of her bare shoulder) hangs on one wall, and on another its companion picture, called "Spring" (another young*

CAPTAIN JINKS

lady, only this one evidently a blonde, also sure of the weather and her health, dressed in a veil and a large bunch of buttercups). On the mantel are some dreadful vases, with nice little bouquets in them, and several photographs and some cards. The stage is empty. The hall door at the back near the double doors opens, and a hotel* Servant shows in* CHARLES LA MARTINE *and* AUGUSTUS VAN VORKENBURG. *The* Servant *carries a small silver tray.*

SERVANT. What names shall I say to Madame Trentoni, gentlemen?

CHARLIE. Simply say two gentlemen. [*He whistles* "Champagne Charlie," *saunters to a window, and pulling aside the lace curtains looks out, as the* Servant *exits.*]

GUSSIE. She's *in* of course! I know that.

CHARLIE. Yes, so do I, but I'll bet you she won't receive us; she'll send word she's out!

GUSSIE [*sitting on the sofa and tracing the cabbage roses on the carpet with his cane*]. I don't see how she dares again. You don't see Captain Jinks coming up the avenue, do you?

CHARLIE. No.

GUSSIE. Oh, but he isn't likely to *miss* a day!

CHARLIE. You're sure it's been every day?

CAPTAIN JINKS

GUSSIE. Yes, or oftener!

CHARLIE [*sits on the piano stool and spins himself around*]. And they're seen constantly everywhere together. Last night it was at Niblo's Garden to see "The Black Crook"! And they're nearly every day at Maillaird's or Delmonico's.

GUSSIE. Well, that'll have to let up a bit after to-night, when she's begun singing.

CHARLIE. You bet. There's not a seat to be had for love or money! They say there's not been such excitement in New York over a début since Jenny Lind.

GUSSIE. Has she been "at home" one single time *you've* called?

CHARLIE. Not one. And you?

GUSSIE. No.

CHARLIE. That's all right! Well, it'll end now, if she sees us to-day. Don't you fail to back me up in everything!

GUSSIE. I'll do my best. Only just as I've learned one lie, you change it; it's very confusing.

The Servant *reënters.*

CHARLIE. *Sh!!*

THE SERVANT. Madame Trentoni cannot say whether she is in or not unless you send up your cards. [*They give the* Servant *their cards, and he again exits.*]

GUSSIE [*examining the photographs on the mantel*]. Who bailed Jinks out of jail that day she landed?

CHARLIE. Mapleson.

GUSSIE. Why did *he?*

CHARLIE. Oh, he always liked Captain Jinks! He likes all us good-looking fellows who make things hum at the Academy. *He* was a bully clever chap, that customs detective!

GUSSIE [*looking through the cards in the card-receiver*]. When does Jinks' case come up in court?

CHARLIE. To-day.

GUSSIE. To-day?

CHARLIE. Yes, this afternoon.

GUSSIE. What time?

CHARLIE. Two o'clock.

GUSSIE. Two o'clock. Good! It'll ruin his chance with Trentoni.

CHARLIE. Don't be an ass! Didn't he get into the scrape to save her inconvenience! it will make a hero of him in her eyes.

GUSSIE [*whistles*]. I didn't think of that! Probably he has told her all about it already.

CHARLIE. Go West, Fitznoodle! he's too damned

modest. Besides, he's clever enough to see that if he told her about it, it would sound infernally like brag, and spoil the effect. By the way, you'll have to lend me another hundred.

GUSSIE. By Jove! that makes a good deal, you know.

CHARLIE. Yes, but I must keep up appearances to catch Trentoni. So you must fork over *more* if you want to get the *rest* back.

GUSSIE. What do you want this hundred for?

CHARLIE. For a new Prince Albert and a swallow-tail suit. Look here; if she sees us now this is what I am going to say to her.

GUSSIE. What?

CHARLIE. That Jinks bet us he would marry her, and would pay his bet out of *her* money.

GUSSIE. But he can deny that.

CHARLIE. Let him, we're two to one!

GUSSIE. But still—

CHARLIE [*interrupting*]. He made *a* bet, didn't he? He'll acknowledge that—I never heard him lie in his life; besides, I have his I O U to prove it. And I intend to arrange things so that he won't know really what he's owning up to. *Sh!*

The Servant *reenters.*

CAPTAIN JINKS

THE SERVANT. Madame Trentoni regrets she is out! [*He places their two cards on top of the card-receiver. There is a knock on the hall door. The* Servant *goes to open it.*]

CHARLIE. Jinks, I'll bet you!

The Servant *opens the door and* Captain JINKS *enters.*

CAPTAIN JINKS. Madame Trentoni? [*Sees the two other men; he is not pleased, and bows coolly to them.*] How are you!

CHARLIE. Madame Trentoni is *out;* we've just sent up our cards.

CAPTAIN JINKS [*giving one of his cards to the* Servant]. Oh, well, perhaps you didn't have *trumps!* Try this one!

THE SERVANT. Yes, sir. [*He goes out.*]

CHARLIE. Well, have you worked it up—your flirtation?

CAPTAIN JINKS [*very quietly*]. No.

CHARLIE. Then what are you doing here?

CAPTAIN JINKS [*firmly*]. That's my affair.

CHARLIE. If you think you are going to marry this lady—

CAPTAIN JINKS [*still quietly but with tension*]. That's *her* affair.

CHARLIE. I'll be damned if you do!

CAPTAIN JINKS. You will be if I *don't*, if it's thanks to *your* interference.

CHARLIE. Have you asked her yet?

CAPTAIN JINKS. Not often enough.

CHARLIE. Have you any reason to believe she will accept you?

CAPTAIN JINKS. None of your business.

CHARLIE [*getting angry and speaking louder*]. Yes, it is, the business of all three of us!

CAPTAIN JINKS [*also getting angry, and less contained*]. Look here, don't you dare mention that damned *wager!*

CHARLIE. You made it!

CAPTAIN JINKS. I called it off! I lost, if you like, and you have my note; in a week it will be paid up. I know when I made that bet appearances were against me, but this woman has taught me I'm not a fool, nor a blackguard, after all. As a fact, I haven't asked her to be my wife yet; but I've come to do so *now*, because *this morning* I got some work to do, an *honest job*, not very elegant—it wouldn't suit either of you—but it'll earn me a living, and thank God it puts me in a position to ask the woman I love to be my wife.

The Servant *comes back.*

CAPTAIN JINKS

THE SERVANT [*to* Captain JINKS]. Madame Trentoni will be down in a few minutes. [*He exits.*]

CAPTAIN JINKS. Thank you.

CHARLIE. Huh!

Captain JINKS *goes to the piano and with the forefinger of his right hand picks out "I'm Captain Jinks of the Horse Marines," playing it with a sort of triumphant force.*

CHARLIE [*to* GUSSIE]. Come along; we might as well take our cards back. [*And going to the card-receiver they take their cards and put them back in their cases.*] We may have to economize! Oh! By Jove! I have one of my clever ideas.

The Servant *goes to the hall door and opening it stands ready to show out* CHARLIE *and* GUSSIE.

CHARLIE [*stops to speak to the* Servant]. Is Professor Belliarti in the hotel?

THE SERVANT. No, sir; I expect he's at the Academy of Music.

CHARLIE. Good! He's our next move. [*To* GUSSIE, *linking his arm in his.*] We'll go there!

They go out. Captain JINKS *looks over his shoulder and seeing them go changes to "Shoo Fly, don't bother me" on the piano, and just as he finishes* AURELIA *enters.*

SKETCH BY PERCY ANDERSON
for *Second Ballet Lady*

CAPTAIN JINKS

AURELIA [*singing*]. "Shoo Fly, don't bother me!"
—that's a civil greeting! [*Laughing.*]

CAPTAIN JINKS. That was for La Martine and Van Vorkenburg.

AURELIA. Oh!—do you know—I don't want to be rude, but I can't bear your friends.

CAPTAIN JINKS. Neither can I.

AURELIA. And by the way, before I forget it, I hope you'll come to supper to-night—here. Will you? After the opera.

CAPTAIN JINKS. Delighted!

AURELIA. No grand powwow! Only one or two distinguished people with the company, and Mapleson, and the Arditis. Oh, yes, and those two nice funny creatures who wanted me to début in oratorio. They've been most kind to Mrs. Gee, and are to be at "Traviata" to-night after all! I'll let you sit between them!

CAPTAIN JINKS [*laughing*]. There's a prize for a good boy.

AURELIA. Won't you sit down? [*Sitting on the piano stool.*]

CAPTAIN JINKS. Won't you take the chair? Let me sit on the piano stool?

AURELIA. No, indeed, you don't wear a bustle. It's

CAPTAIN JINKS

the only comfortable seat for me in the room! It was very kind of you to call this noon. I hoped you would, but—

CAPTAIN JINKS [*pulling his chair nearer her*]. "But?" It was an appointment!

AURELIA. Oh, yes, but I can never be certain. You remember our very first appointment you deliberately *broke!* [*Teasingly.*]

CAPTAIN JINKS. You mean that day you landed?

AURELIA. You promised to come to the hotel at four o'clock.

CAPTAIN JINKS. Oh, yes, but you forgave me for that long ago, when I told you I was *detained—in more senses than one!* And very unavoidably, not to mention unwillingly!

AURELIA. But you never told me why.

CAPTAIN JINKS. No, I couldn't, but I will *some* day. Are you nervous about to-night?

AURELIA. Frightfully!

CAPTAIN JINKS. You'll take the roof off the Academy!

AURELIA. I *hae me doots!* I'm not so sure I'm not an acquired taste, like olives and tomatoes and Russian caviare! But tell me one thing—

CAPTAIN JINKS. I'm going to before I leave this

room. [*He changes his seat to a chair close beside the piano.*]

AURELIA. Really! What?

CAPTAIN JINKS. No, let's have yours first. When I get started on mine there won't be time for anything else.

AURELIA. Well—supposing—by some heaven-sent chance—I do succeed, even like in London; then you know, after I've bowed thirty-two times, with a heaving bosom, and thrown kisses like fireworks to the gallery twenty-three times, if they still keep on,—and oh, goodness, how I love them when they do!—then I sing something, just some little song. Now I want to sing "Home, Sweet Home." Do you know it?

CAPTAIN JINKS. Oh, yes. Clara Louise Kellogg sings it on the same occasions.

AURELIA. With variations? I have trills and all sorts of monkey tricks!

CAPTAIN JINKS. So has she!

AURELIA. I was afraid so. Well, then, I think I'll sing a little song called "The Last Rose of Summer." [*She sings a bar or two.*] Have you heard it? [*She sings the verse through.*]

CAPTAIN JINKS. No.

AURELIA. It's quite new and unhackneyed, isn't

CAPTAIN JINKS

it? I sing it in "Martha."

CAPTAIN JINKS. Not very lively though! Why not sing "Those Tassels on her Boots"?

AURELIA [*laughing*]. I don't know it; show me! [*Getting up from the piano stool she makes him sit down and sing.* Captain JINKS *sings one verse, accompanying himself with his forefinger.*] Entrancing! Only I don't think the Anti-French Literature League would approve of the sentiment!

CAPTAIN JINKS [*turning on the stool, rises, and speaks seriously*]. There would be just *one* consolation to me if you did n't make a success at all!

AURELIA. You horrid brute! There would be *no* consolation for me.

CAPTAIN JINKS. That is *my* misfortune—

AURELIA. Really! How do you mean?—

CAPTAIN JINKS. It would make it so much easier for me to ask you to marry me!

A knock on the hall door.

AURELIA. Well, then, let's *pretend* I've failed!

PETER, *the newsboy, in the livery of a hotel servant, enters.*

CAPTAIN JINKS. Hello, Peter!

PETER. Hello, sir!

CAPTAIN JINKS. How do you like your new job?

CAPTAIN JINKS

PETER. Oh, it ain't bad— [*Aside to* Captain JINKS.] I does it for *her* sake, so as to be near *her*, but I find it very confining.

AURELIA. What is it, Peter?

PETER. Beg pardon, ma'am, the reporter from the Tribune wants to see you on a personal matter of great importance.

AURELIA. Say I'm out.

PETER. Yes, ma'am. [*Exits.*]

AURELIA. What a horrid moment to be interrupted in. *Please* go on *just* where you left off!

CAPTAIN JINKS. You are very rich and popular and beautiful and all the rest of it— [*He stops.*]

AURELIA [*childishly happy and delighted*]. Oh, that is n't fair! to hurry through with just "all the rest of it." I wonder you did n't say I was beautiful *et cetera!* No siree! You must enumerate singly every solitary nice thing you think I am!

CAPTAIN JINKS. It would take too long!

AURELIA. How long?

CAPTAIN JINKS. The rest of my life! [*Starting to embrace her. Another knock on the hall door. They start apart and sit on opposite sides of the table. Then* AURELIA *speaks.*]

AURELIA. Come in.

CAPTAIN JINKS

PETER *reënters.*

PETER. Please, ma'am, the reporter from the Tribune told me to ask you, so long as you was dead set on being out, if the news was true what has come to his office, that you was engaged to be married to *him?* [*Pointing to* Captain JINKS.]

AURELIA [*on one side of the table*]. It won't be true if he keeps on interrupting with messages all the day! You tell the gentleman, Peter, that I've gone to the Academy.

CAPTAIN JINKS [*on the other side of the table*]. And if he asks you anything about me tell him you don't know who I am.

PETER. Oh, but I can't.

CAPTAIN JINKS. Why not?

PETER. 'Cause I've just told him you've been to see Madame Trentoni every day!

AURELIA. What did you do that for?

PETER. For a dollar!

CAPTAIN JINKS. That's a nice return to make to Madame Trentoni for getting you this good position in a high-toned hotel!

PETER. If you wanted me to lie about it you ought ter have told me; I thought it was something she'd be proud of.

AURELIA. That's all right, Peter; go give my mes-

CAPTAIN JINKS

sage and don't answer any more questions about me at all.

PETER. Yes, ma'am. [*Exits.*]

AURELIA. Peter wasn't so far wrong; I'm not ashamed of your visits.

CAPTAIN JINKS [*rises and goes to her*]. Look here, I'm not worth your little finger, but if you'll only overlook my beastly unworthiness and just let my love for you count, I'll do my best so long as I live to make my wife the happiest woman in the world.

AURELIA. But I'm *nobody*.

CAPTAIN JINKS. The woman I love—*nobody?*

AURELIA. But your family—your mother—?

CAPTAIN JINKS. *You* are the woman I love.

AURELIA. Still I mayn't be the woman your mother loves!

CAPTAIN JINKS. Oh, well, say! Are you marrying mother or *me?*

AURELIA. But won't your mother be shocked at your marrying a "lady on the stage"?

CAPTAIN JINKS [*half amused*]. Oh, very likely she'll carry on awful for a while! The Ladies' Anti-French Literature League is *broad-minded* compared to mother! But she's an angel all the same; and as birds of a feather flock together, she will soon chum up with *you* when she has once had a chance to know you.

AURELIA. I'm not so sure. She'll think you are going to perdition!

CAPTAIN JINKS. Oh, no, to a much hotter place! But when she *knows you!*

AURELIA. You think so, because you think you are in love with me.

CAPTAIN JINKS. "Think!"

AURELIA [*rising*]. It would break my heart to come between you and your mother.

CAPTAIN JINKS. Now, don't be selfish; it will break mine if you refuse me, and you'd rather break your heart than mine, wouldn't you? [*Coming close to her.*]

AURELIA [*teasing, and backing slowly away*]. Oh, I don't know.—

CAPTAIN JINKS [*following her*]. Madame Trentoni!—Oh, can't I call you something else, something more friendly, more personal?

AURELIA. Yes, you may call me—Miss Johnson; that's my real name, you know!—

CAPTAIN JINKS. But you have another, a nearer one—

AURELIA. Oh, well, go on with Miss Johnson for a few minutes.—

CAPTAIN JINKS

CAPTAIN JINKS [*makes her let him take her hand*]. Listen to me seriously. This is a question for *you* and *me* to decide. Let's decide it now! Do you know that until I met you I was a lazy good-for-nothing loafer! Now, I'm afraid I'm not good for much, but I'm no longer lazy, and I'm a lover instead of a loafer! Let me work for you, will you? It's no fun working only for myself! Make my dreams come true, just to prove the rule that they don't.

AURELIA. There are dreams—and *dreams!*—

CAPTAIN JINKS. Yes, but mine are all alike, day dreams and all, full of one idea, one desire,—your love. I can't express myself; I don't know how to say it, but what I mean is that I don't want to go anywhere, on sea, on land, in the city, in the country, anywhere, unless *you* are there beside me. Life without you doesn't seem worth the trouble! Oh! If I only dared hope you could care a little for a chap like me.

AURELIA [*softening, and with bent head, looks at him sweetly from the corner of her eye*]. I give you permission to *dream* that!

CAPTAIN JINKS. Really?

AURELIA. Yes, and you can even make the "*little*" a *good deal!*—

CAPTAIN JINKS. You— [*Interrupted. **He** is going to say "darling."*]

CAPTAIN JINKS

AURELIA. Wait a minute! You know I'm not really half so nice as you think I am.

CAPTAIN JINKS. Are n't you? —

AURELIA. No, but it won't make any difference, if you never find it out! Only, suppose I were to fail to-night—

CAPTAIN JINKS. Ah! That's just what I meant by having one consolation; you would know then I loved you only for your dear self, and if you loved me, we could say, "Never mind, for *love* does n't fail!"

AURELIA [*with tears in her eyes*]. You *are* a darling— [*A knock on the hall door. They change their places quickly.* Captain JINKS *sits again on one side of the centre-table, and* AURELIA *on the other. They exchange a smiling glance of understanding as* AURELIA *says* "*Come in.*"]

PETER *enters*.

PETER. Ice water! [*He rattles the ice in a white china pitcher which he places between them on the centre-table.* AURELIA *and* Captain JINKS *exchange hopeless glances.*] The chambermaid wants to know if she can come in and do this room now?

AURELIA. No, she can't! [*She goes to the writing-desk and writes in ink with the wrong end of a pen on a big sheet of fresh white blotting-paper there.*]

CAPTAIN JINKS [*taking* PETER *to one side by the*

SKETCH BY PERCY ANDERSON
for *Fourth Ballet Lady—"Miss Hochspitz"*

CAPTAIN JINKS

collar of his coat]. Look here, if you bring any more messages, or ice water, or reporters, or chambermaids, or any other damned thing to Madame Trentoni this afternoon, I'll break your neck! Do you understand?

PETER. No, sir!

CAPTAIN JINKS. Well, think it over as you go downstairs.

PETER. What's it worth?

CAPTAIN JINKS. Your *neck*, that's all—go on, git!

PETER. Yes, sir. [*Half-way to the door, he stops.*] Say! I'll bet you a quarter, no one gets into this room what ain't wanted!

CAPTAIN JINKS. All right!

PETER. Thank you! [*He exits, happy.* AURELIA *follows him to the door with the blotting-paper, which she holds in front of her, displaying it to* Captain JINKS.]

AURELIA. There! How would it do if I put *this* on the door? [*The paper reads in large black letters* "*Engaged.*"]

CAPTAIN JINKS. It would be all right if you would add "to R. Jinks."

AURELIA [*laughing*]. How dare you! Certainly *not!*

CAPTAIN JINKS. Why?

AURELIA. Because— [*Closing the door she turns*

and faces him.] Because— [*She comes slowly to him.*] Because it's the truth!

CAPTAIN JINKS [*embracing her*]. You *love* me! [*In his arms, she doesn't answer.*] *Do you* love me? [*Still in his arms, she doesn't answer.*] You don't answer?

AURELIA [*looking up at him*]. Am I trying to get out of your arms?

CAPTAIN JINKS. Darling!

AURELIA. *Yours!* [*She bursts into tears.*]

CAPTAIN JINKS [*frightened*]. Dearest, what's the matter? You are crying!—

AURELIA. I know it, I'm *so happy!*

Papa BELLIARTI *comes in unannounced. He brings with him his violin in a green baize bag.*

PROFESSOR BELLIARTI. Bless my stars and ballet dancers! Ought I have knocked! [AURELIA *and* Captain JINKS *have broken quickly from each other's arms.*]

CAPTAIN JINKS. Oh, no, we're *accustomed* to interruptions this morning!

PROFESSOR BELLIARTI [*to* AURELIA]. Having a little rehearsal with a new tenor, my dear? [*Placing the bag on the piano—busy with his violin.*]

AURELIA [*laughing*]. Yes, sort of like that?

PROFESSOR BELLIARTI. The ladies of the ballet are here to rehearse at your request, you know.

CAPTAIN JINKS

AURELIA. O dear, that's true. I forgot. You'll have to excuse me, Captain Jinks.

CAPTAIN JINKS [*bows to* AURELIA, *and turning to* Professor BELLIARTI *offers him a cigar very pleasantly.*] Have a cigar?

PROFESSOR BELLIARTI. Thank you! [*Takes one and puts it in his pocket.*] Ahem! [*Turning his back, pointedly, he takes up his violin, which is in perfect tune, and tunes it, with a smile on his face, but only his friendly back toward* AURELIA *and* Captain JINKS.]

CAPTAIN JINKS [*to* AURELIA]. Shan't I tell him?

AURELIA. I think he'd rather *I* told him—he's such a dear sensitive old thing!

CAPTAIN JINKS. And then afterwards *I* will ask his consent; don't you think that would please him?

AURELIA. Oh, yes, do. It will make him feel he is something to both of us! How nice of you to have the idea! Come back in quarter of an hour.

CAPTAIN JINKS. It's one o'clock; I'll be back on the minute of fifteen past! But I won't be able to stay, for I have an engagement, at *two*, that must not be put off.

AURELIA [*happy, and smiling*]. Oh, I'll excuse you!—

CAPTAIN JINKS [*stopping, and looking into her*

eyes a moment]. *This is no dream?* You're sure I'm awake?

AURELIA. Let's see! [*She looks around first at* Papa BELLIARTI, *whom she sees still has his back turned, and then, leaning over, she kisses* Captain JINKS.] How is it?—Awake?

CAPTAIN JINKS. Not sure yet—try again.

AURELIA [*laughing*]. No *siree!!* Good-by—[*Giving him her hand, which he presses.*]

CAPTAIN JINKS. Good-by. [*He starts to go. At the door he hesitates and stands looking at* AURELIA. *She slowly joins him at the door, questioningly.*] Are you sure whether *you're* awake or not?

AURELIA. *Quite sure!* But I may be uncertain in fifteen minutes!

CAPTAIN JINKS. Don't ask *Papa Belliarti* then, *I'll* be back!

AURELIA. Papa Belliarti!

PROFESSOR BELLIARTI [*with his back still turned*]. Has he gone?

AURELIA. Yes, you silly old goose! [*Going to him, takes him lovingly by the shoulders.*] Turn around!

PROFESSOR BELLIARTI. So my singing bird is caught at last, eh! [*She hides her happy blushing face in his arms.*] I'm very glad! [*He speaks this latter sentence with tears in his voice and eyes.*] Very

—glad, for her sake! But I'll miss you, little girl!—

AURELIA. It isn't to make any difference to you at all! Let me tell you—

PROFESSOR BELLIARTI. Sh! Not now. Mrs. Gee is coming; I sent for her to accompany me on the piano for the ballet ladies.

Mrs. GREENBOROUGH *enters at this moment through the double doors at back.*

MRS. GREENBOROUGH. Good afternoon, everybody. Papa Belliarti sent for me, Aurelia, to—

PROFESSOR BELLIARTI. I told her, madam.

MRS. GREENBOROUGH [*looking around room, under the sofa, behind the chairs, and even absent-mindedly on the piano and mantelpiece*]. Aurelia, I can't find my bustle anywhere; I believe that chambermaid has stolen it!

AURELIA. Dear heart! If you had any more bustle I don't know where you'd put it!

MRS. GREENBOROUGH. Oh, well, of course I had to have a makeshift, so I took all those nice newspapers that had our arrival in.

AURELIA. You both know why I've had these dancers come! I want everything to-night as near perfection as possible! No rough edges, no horrid slip-ups! And the dancing at yesterday's rehearsal was awful! How many ladies are coming, Papa?

CAPTAIN JINKS

Professor Belliarti. Seven — the leads!

Aurelia. Good! If *they're* all right, the others can't go wrong. I have especial reasons *besides it being my New York début why I want everything to-night to be perfect!* Haven't I, Papa Belliarti? [*Whispers to him.*] Shall I tell her, Papa?

Mrs. Greenborough [*curious*]. Well, now, Aurelia, I consider you're real tantalizing if you have secrets — [*Interrupted.*]

Aurelia. If you keep on talking, dear heart, I can never tell you.

Mrs. Greenborough. *Talking! Me!* It's twenty years since I've spoken one complete sentence of any length, all the way through.

Aurelia. Well, then, to make up, I'll tell you. Stand over there! [*Placing her.*] Lean against the table, so as to have some support if you should feel faint! There! [*Having bolstered* Mrs. Greenborough *against the centre-table, she crosses the room to* Papa Belliarti *and takes his arm. They stand facing* Mrs. Greenborough. Professor Belliarti *hums a few bars of the Mendelssohn wedding march, and they slowly approach* Mrs. Greenborough.]

Mrs. Greenborough. Good gracious, I hope — [*Interrupted.*]

Aurelia. Ssh! — Papa Belliarti and I are very happy!

AURELIA. Papa Belliarti and I are very happy!

CAPTAIN JINKS

PROFESSOR BELLIARTI. What?

AURELIA. Well— *Are n't you?*

PROFESSOR BELLIARTI. Yes, dear. Yes! Of course —only!

MRS. GREENBOROUGH [*excited*]. Do go on, I 'm eaten up with curiosity, I 'm guessing— [*Interrupted.*]

AURELIA. You 're guessing wrong! I 'm going to be married.

MRS. GREENBOROUGH. Bless my soul! To Papa Belliarti!

PROFESSOR BELLIARTI. That 's a crazy idea!

AURELIA. No! No! Go on with your guessing! Who is it?

MRS. GREENBOROUGH. Dear heart, I *can't* guess!

AURELIA. Catch me, and I 'll tell you! [*She runs, gaily laughing, around the table, then around a big armchair, and then around* Papa BELLIARTI, Mrs. GREENBOROUGH *running after her and talking all the time.* AURELIA *dodges around* Papa BELLIARTI, *turns suddenly, and herself catches* Mrs. GREENBOROUGH *and gives her a hug and a kiss. Then she drags her over to the piano, plumps her down on the piano stool facing the keys, and leaning over her back with her own hands on the piano plays "Captain Jinks."*] *Now!* Can't you guess?

CAPTAIN JINKS

MRS. GREENBOROUGH [*gives a little high scream of delight*]. Eeh! It's the young man who gave me the booky the day we landed!

AURELIA [*hugging her delightedly around the neck*]. Of course! Do you suppose there is another man in this whole world I'd marry!

MRS. GREENBOROUGH. I *thought* he liked us that very day!

AURELIA. I'm so happy! I'm no Prima Donna now, I'm only a girl, and the happiest girl that ever was! Listen! You two dear people think I've been singing these last two years, don't you! Wait till you hear me to-night! You'll say I never sang before! There's only one man in this world for me, and I'm going to marry him! [*She hugs* Professor BELLIARTI *impulsively*.] What do you think of that for *real* JOY!

There is a knock on the hall door.

AURELIA. Come in! Come in, *everybody!*

PETER *enters*.

PETER. Please, ma'am, there's a party of females says they has an engagement with you. I thought they was kiddin', so I wouldn't let 'm in till I asted you.

PROFESSOR BELLIARTI. The Ballet Ladies!

AURELIA. Show them up, Peter; they're *artistes!*

CAPTAIN JINKS

PETER. They're right here. [*He calls into hall.*] Come along in! [*And goes out after they have entered.*]

The Seven Ballet Ladies *enter. Three are young and pretty. Three are about fifty; one of these three is rather stout and one is very thin. The seventh is inclined to* embonpoint *also, but bravely restricted at every curve. She hails from the Paris Opera. The thin one is a widow and wears a widow's weeds. Her dress is a trifle short and shows a hair's-breadth escape of white stocking above her prunella boots. She brings with her, leading by the hand, a small child. Her offspring is dressed in white piqué, and wears pantalettes and goloshes. They all say "good day." Two of the younger ones are rather free and impertinent in their manner, the others are somewhat embarrassed; all carry little bags or parcels supposed to contain their ballet dresses. The widow's is done up in an old newspaper.*

AURELIA. How do you do, ladies!

They all bow and murmur again a greeting.

PROFESSOR BELLIARTI. Madame Trentoni wants to have the performance perfection to-night, and so she thought a little quiet rehearsal of the principal ladies of the ballet here, with her, a good thing all around.

AURELIA. You did beautifully last night, but you know this new rose figure Professor Belliarti is teaching you is very difficult, and if there is the slightest mistake it is ruined.

There is a nervous movement of all the Seven, *several clearing their throats, others slightly changing their position from one foot to the other. One or two, including the widow, look very supercilious, as if to say,* "O *dear me! think of* her *telling us what* is *and what* ain't *easy!* us, *who are old enough to be her grandmother!" Though I'm sure they would n't have put it in just that way. They would probably have spoken of her as a "raw amateur," and of themselves as "trained* artistes."

PROFESSOR BELLIARTI [*opening the folding doors at the back, shows the big empty room*]. We may use this room too if we need it to dance in.

The Ballet Ladies *look in its direction.*

AURELIA. We're all going to try our very best, are n't we, to-night?

THE THIRD BALLET LADY [*with a curtsey*]. Si, si, Signora.

THE SIXTH BALLET LADY [*the widow*]. Oh, it'll be hall roight. There ain't no trouble with that polka step!

THE FOURTH BALLET LADY. Dat vas nicht ein polka shtep!

THE FIRST BALLET LADY [*Miss Pettitoes*]. Yes, it was!

CAPTAIN JINKS

The Fourth Ballet Lady. Nein! Nein! I dell you dat vas ein— [*Interrupted.*]

Professor Belliarti [*firmly*]. Ladies!

The Fourth Ballet Lady. Dat vos nicht ein polka shtep!

The First Ballet Lady. Miss Hochspitz is always quarrelling, sir; that's why she had to leave Germany and come over here!

The Fourth Ballet Lady. Och Himmel! Dat vos not drue, mein herr! She is von *cat*, dis Caroline Peddidoes!

Professor Belliarti. Come, come, Fraulein, remember I always insist on my ballet being a happy family.

Miss Hochspitz *pinches* Miss Pettitoes. *Miss* Pettitoes *slaps* Miss Hochspitz's *face. All the Ballet Ladies join in and there is a general quarrel.*

Aurelia. Ladies! *please* do remember we engage you to dance, not to *sing!* We'll do all the squabbling ourselves! You have some things with you to rehearse in?

The Sixth Ballet Lady. Oh, yes, miss, we've hall got combing jackets and hour regular re'earsing costumes, the rest of the way down.

They all show their bundles.

Aurelia. Where'll they change?

CAPTAIN JINKS

PROFESSOR BELLIARTI. In here. [*Motioning to the big room at back.*]

MRS. GREENBOROUGH. No; let them come to my room.

AURELIA. They can't go through the hall after they're dressed!

MRS. GREENBOROUGH. They don't have to; that door to the right [*pointing off in the big room*] opens into a private passage which connects straight with my room. It's the way I always come.

AURELIA. Very well, then, ladies, please, if you will kindly go with Mrs. Greenborough.

MRS. GREENBOROUGH. Follow me, etc. —

She leads the way, talking, followed by the Seven Ballet Ladies, *the widow still leading her child.* BELLIARTI *closes the door after them. Then he comes slowly to* AURELIA, *watching her with a sweet smile. When he reaches her he takes her two hands.*

PROFESSOR BELLIARTI. I'm as happy as you, my dear. There's only one worry — is he worthy of you?

AURELIA. He's worth a dozen of me, voice and all!

PROFESSOR BELLIARTI [*sitting in the big armchair by the table*]. Still, he is all the time with one gay company of young men who lead what you call *very quick lives!* So let old Papa Belliarti poke

(98)

CAPTAIN JINKS

about a little and ask a few questions before you make the engagement public, will you?

AURELIA. If you want to. You will be proud, I know, of all you hear! Women, dear Papa, are perfect barometers for a good and bad man! [*She sits on the floor at his feet and lays her head on his knees.*]

PROFESSOR BELLIARTI. And nothing gets out of order like a barometer! They're always pointing to Fair Weather when it's raining cats and dogs!

AURELIA [*laughing*]. True; but when you hear me sing to-night, you'll acknowledge that I am in perfect condition!

PROFESSOR BELLIARTI [*leaning over and putting his arm about her neck*]. I hope so. And I hope your new life, my dear, will be one long happy dance. Not the new-fangled step, this polka redowa, for that is a love at first sight that will die a violent death, exhausted before the honeymoon is over! Not the waltz, for a waltz with us must need have some reverses, and I want no reverses in my little girl's life; not a Virginia reel, for that entails long separations from one's partner, and a flirtatious swinging of *all* the men down the line; but I would have your life's dance the minuet, which is not so fast as to tire you out, whose music is Mozart's, —our best—a dance where you and your partner are never long separated, and where you mingle with your amusement a certain graceful graciousness toward each other which will keep familiarity forever from breeding contempt.

AURELIA [*with a choke in her voice*]. Our life shall be a minuet, dear father, and you must teach us *both our steps.*

A knock on the hall door.

PROFESSOR BELLIARTI [*rising*]. Come in!

AURELIA *also rises.* PETER *enters.*

PETER. Two lardy-dah gents to see *you,* and an old lady for *you,* ma'am. [*Giving cards to* Professor BELLIARTI *and one to* AURELIA.]

PROFESSOR BELLIARTI [*reading his cards*]. Mr. Charles La Martine and Mr. Van Vorkenburg?

PETER. Them's the two what always finds Madame Trenton out! They've been to the theaytre after you, and they says it's important.

AURELIA [*with suppressed happiness and proudly*]. See who my visitor is! [*Shows* Papa BELLIARTI *her card.*]

PROFESSOR BELLIARTI [*reading card*]. Who is it, his mother?

AURELIA. It must be! Come already to congratulate me! He never even told me she was here, and we were both rather afraid of her.

CAPTAIN JINKS

PETER. Well, are *you* out to them gents too?

PROFESSOR BELLIARTI. No, show them to my room, and say I'll be with them immediately.

PETER [*to* AURELIA]. And the old party?

AURELIA [*with pointed emphasis*]. Show the *distinguished lady* here at once!

PETER. Gee! [*And with his tongue in his cheek, he exits.*]

PROFESSOR BELLIARTI. She'll be a proud mother when she sees you. I hope to be back in time to be presented to her.

AURELIA [*half teasing*]. I don't know if she'll approve of you, Papa! She's against *acting!*

PROFESSOR BELLIARTI. *Dancing* is a *higher art!*

AURELIA. So it is, sometimes! [*They both laugh.*]

PROFESSOR BELLIARTI. Margaret Fuller and Ralph Waldo Emerson were once discussing Fanny Elssler. "It isn't dancing, Margaret, it's poetry," said Emerson. "My dear Ralph," back spoke Miss Fuller, "it's not poetry, it's *religion.*"

A delicate knock is heard on the hall door.

AURELIA [*a little frightened*]. There she is!

Professor BELLIARTI *opens the door, bowing low.* Mrs. JINKS *enters.* Professor BELLIARTI, *bowing, goes out, closing the door after him.* Mrs. JINKS *is an*

CAPTAIN JINKS

elderly, sweetly severe, delicate-featured little woman, dressed in rich light brown silk, but in a past fashion. She wears full spreading skirts, and carries a small parasol to match her dress.

MRS. JINKS [*inclining her head with a serious, dignified grace*]. Madame Trentoni?

AURELIA [*with a low curtsey*]. Yes, madam. You have heard? [Mrs. JINKS *bows her head in acquiescence.*] How good of you to come so soon! Ah! I must kiss you.

MRS. JINKS. *Please don't!*

AURELIA [*kissing her*]. I do so want you to love me.

MRS. JINKS [*like a stone statue when she is kissed, and showing no flurry*]. Forgive me, but I extremely dislike demonstrative people!

AURELIA. I'm so sorry. Will you sit down?

MRS. JINKS [*with a quiet and firm though sweet voice, very serious and rather haughty*]. Thank you, I would rather stand. [AURELIA *looks up frightened.*] I am afraid the reason for my visit is not a pleasant one. By all means, however, sit down yourself.

AURELIA [*at once on the defensive*]. Oh, no, I shall stand if you do!

MRS. JINKS. My son does not yet know of my

SKETCH BY PERCY ANDERSON
for *Sixth Ballet Lady*—"*Mrs. Maggitt*"

arrival, but I received a letter from him the other day saying he intended asking you to marry him. I've not slept a wink since!

AURELIA. I regret that your night's rest has been disturbed.

MRS. JINKS. Hoping to reach you before he takes so fatal a step, to assure you such a thing is impossible, I took the first train.

AURELIA. I'm afraid you took a *slow* one, for you are too late!

MRS. JINKS. He's already proposed?

AURELIA. And been accepted! Not half an hour ago. [Mrs. JINKS *closes her eyes as if she were going to faint and sinks into a chair.*] Don't, please, take it so to heart! Please —

MRS. JINKS. Pardon me, I don't mean to be rude. This marriage cannot take place. *You must* give him up.

AURELIA. It is quite impossible! I am no *Camille*, madam! [*Sitting determinedly at the opposite side of the table.*]

MRS. JINKS. No what?

AURELIA. No *Marguerite Gautier*.

MRS. JINKS. I do not know the lady.

AURELIA [*bitterly*]. Oh, she wouldn't move in

CAPTAIN JINKS

your set! But don't you remember the scene in the play "Camille," where she gives up the lover to satisfy his father? It ruined both their lives.

MRS. JINKS. I never go to the theatre.

AURELIA. That's a pity, because I am sure if you did you would not be giving us both this painful experience. Well, I am a good woman, Mrs. Jinks, and I love your son.

MRS. JINKS [*pointedly*]. You are also an *actress*, I believe?

AURELIA. Well, there's a difference of opinions about that! but I *am* an Opera Singer, and not ashamed of it!

MRS. JINKS. The Jinkses have never been connected with any profession, except the *Church!*

AURELIA. Every little while the Church and Stage come plump together like that, and I think it does them both good!

MRS. JINKS. The Jinkses are an old and distinguished family; and yours?

AURELIA. I'm doing my honest best to make it distinguished.

MRS. JINKS. But you must acknowledge the thing you threaten doing is n't done. Your bringing up, your lives—everything is at a variance! Happiness is *impossible!*

CAPTAIN JINKS

AURELIA. I disagree with you so long as our hearts are in accord!

MRS. JINKS. Listen. My brother has nearly arranged for a magnificent diplomatic position for my son, his nephew, in the event of Greeley's election, which is certain, of course. This marriage with you will make such a career impossible—ruin his chances—shatter all our hopes for the future!

AURELIA [*rising*]. Madam, I am not much more than a girl, but really—

MRS. JINKS. You *look* very young, but they say you stage women do wonderful things with your cosmetics.

AURELIA. When I am a certain age I may resort to them. [Mrs. JINKS *rises offended.*] You do not realize what sort of a woman you are speaking to. As I started to say, I am young, but I have a will of my own and a heart of my own, in which your son has told me his happiness lies. Loving him as I do and believing in him, I shall not think of insulting his *manhood* by proposing to release him from his engagement.

MRS. JINKS. You will separate me from my son?

AURELIA [*goes a little nearer her*]. No, indeed. I will share him with you. His mother's love remains yours.

CAPTAIN JINKS

MRS. JINKS. I have not yet seen my son. I shall appeal to the mother-love you speak of. [*Starting to go.*]

AURELIA. May I give you a hint? Don't say horrid things about *me!* For if he's the man I think him, that would only steel his heart against you.

MRS. JINKS. He's cried his baby troubles out on my knees, and his boy's sorrows out in my arms! He shall empty his man's heart into my arms too!

AURELIA. Dear me! If he does that, I'm afraid you'll find them rather full; for *I* was all his *man's heart* held half an hour ago!

MRS. JINKS. You are frivolous! Good-by, madam.

AURELIA. No! don't go like that.

MRS. JINKS. Will you give my boy up?

AURELIA. No!

Mrs. JINKS *makes an inclination of the head. She is about to exit, but meets* Professor BELLIARTI *coming in.* Professor BELLIARTI *is very excited, which feeling he tries to control on seeing* Mrs. JINKS.

AURELIA. Oh, Papa Belliarti, I'm glad you've come down. I want to present you to *Mrs. Jinks*, my *future husband's mother!* Mrs. Jinks, Professor Belliarti, my foster-father and the *Ballet Master* of our Opera Company! [Professor BELLIARTI *bows low.*

CAPTAIN JINKS

Mrs. JINKS *closes her eyes and gasps, then giving the merest inclination of her head, she exits.* AURELIA, *excited, slams the door after her.*] She came after my happiness, but she didn't get it! Tell Mrs. Greenborough to bring the ladies in now!

PROFESSOR BELLIARTI. Not yet—not yet! Papa Belliarti is after your happiness too, but to save it for you, to save it for you.

AURELIA. What is it? What's the matter? No accident?

PROFESSOR BELLIARTI. You mustn't marry this Captain Jinks.

AURELIA. *You* too!

PROFESSOR BELLIARTI. He's a blackguard!

AURELIA. Papa! that's not true! How dare you! [Professor BELLIARTI *pours forth a flood of Italian, speaking rapidly and with great excitement and emotion.* AURELIA *stops him, taking hold of his arm and holding it tightly, but affectionately.*] Speak English! *Speak English!* You know I can't understand Italian when you are excited! What do you mean? Does he, like his mother, want to back out?

PROFESSOR BELLIARTI [*grimly*]. Oh, no, not he! Not he! [*Speaking the last "not he" very angrily.*]

AURELIA. Then how dared you call him—[*Interrupted.*]

CAPTAIN JINKS

PROFESSOR BELLIARTI. He is marrying you for your money! For what *you* will *make* for him!

AURELIA. I don't believe it!

PROFESSOR BELLIARTI. He made one bet he would marry you after these young men told him they had heard from Mrs. Gee that you were rich. He made one bet with La Martine and Van Vorkenburg that he would marry you!

AURELIA. I tell you I don't believe it!

PROFESSOR BELLIARTI. A thousand dollars he bet them! Even Mapleson knows it.

AURELIA. Papa! you did n't tell *Mapleson?*

PROFESSOR BELLIARTI. He heard it from a reporter.

AURELIA. It's in the papers?

PROFESSOR BELLIARTI. No. The reporter is a nice gentleman. He was told by a newsboy on the dock the day you landed, but never printed it.

AURELIA. But I don't believe the story. I tell you it is n't *true!* Captain Jinks *never* made such a bet!

PROFESSOR BELLIARTI. I have proof, and I intend to ask him to his face!

AURELIA. Yes; do that, Papa! I'm not afraid of his answer.

PROFESSOR BELLIARTI. *But* if he says he *did* bet so?

SKETCH BY PERCY ANDERSON
for *Sixth Ballet Lady's Child — Miss Victoria Alberta Maggitt*

CAPTAIN JINKS

AURELIA. *Don't let* him say it!

PROFESSOR BELLIARTI. I will make him speak the *truth*, and if he confess he did make that bet you must *not* marry him. He would break your heart, darling, before the honeymoon was over.

A knock on the hall door, but neither hear it.

AURELIA. Oh, no, it's too great an insult. I *know* he isn't capable!

Another knock and then PETER *enters.*

PETER. *Please*, are you all deaf? Captain Jinks is here again and says you're all expecting him, but I wouldn't let him up till I asted.

PROFESSOR BELLIARTI. Send Captain Jinks straight here.

PETER. Yes, sir. Golly! [*Exits.*]

AURELIA. *I* couldn't ask him.

PROFESSOR BELLIARTI. You needn't. But will you give me permission to break off your engagement?

AURELIA. *If* it's true. But I *know* it isn't!

PROFESSOR BELLIARTI [*pointing to the room at the back*]. Go in there. Listen to what we say, and when it is sufficient in your eyes to break off everything between us, make some signal—drop this book. [*Taking a book from the table.*]

AURELIA [*going to the door, she turns there*]. Ask

him outright if he made the bet—and be sure he says "*No*" loud. [*She goes into the other room and closes the doors behind her.*]

PROFESSOR BELLIARTI. If wishing could only make him turn out to be worthy of my girl!—[*A knock on the hall door. He pulls himself together.*] Come in. [Captain JINKS *dashes in very happy and expectant.*]

CAPTAIN JINKS. Ah, sir! The very man I wanted to see!

PROFESSOR BELLIARTI. And *me* too.

CAPTAIN JINKS. I have a *most* important question to ask you!

PROFESSOR BELLIARTI. *Me too!*

CAPTAIN JINKS. Have a cigar? [*Offering one.*]

PROFESSOR BELLIARTI. No, thank you! And here's the one back you gave me a little while ago. [*Giving the cigar from his pocket.*]

CAPTAIN JINKS [*taking the cigar, rather perplexed and not understanding*]. Have a chair? [*Offering one, and about to sit himself.*]

PROFESSOR BELLIARTI. No! [Captain JINKS, *about to sit down—does n't.*]

CAPTAIN JINKS. Ah, well then, straight to the point, Signor Belliarti. [*Bowing elaborately, mock-*

CAPTAIN JINKS

ing, happy.] Will you give me your adopted daughter to be my wife?

Professor Belliarti. *Yes!* if you will give me your word of honor you didn't sign that paper! [*Giving him, with trembling hand, the paper* Captain Jinks *signed in Act I.*]

Captain Jinks. *What paper?* [*Taking paper from* Belliarti—*aghast.*] By Jove! My I O U! How did you get hold of this?

Professor Belliarti. Good Lord! You know what it is? Then you *did* sign it? You're a blackguard, sir, to try and cheat my child!

Captain Jinks [*throws the paper on to the table*]. Hold on a minute! Hold on! You're an old man and I can't treat you as I would a younger, but you must take that "blackguard" back!

Professor Belliarti. Never! If it's true you made this wager about my little girl. Forget my age if you like, but I *won't* take "blackguard" back!

Captain Jinks. Yes, you will, if it's a lie! Where is Madame Trentoni? I want to see her herself.

Professor Belliarti. First answer me my question. Is that your signature? Did you make that wager?

Captain Jinks [*after a moment's pause, ashamed*]. Yes— [*Again a moment's pause; the book is dropped*

CAPTAIN JINKS

by AURELIA *in the next room and is distinctly heard as it strikes the floor. The sound rouses* Captain JINKS *and* Professor BELLIARTI.] But— [*Interrupted.*]

PROFESSOR BELLIARTI [*beside himself*]. *Not one other word, sir!* I am asked by Madame Trentoni to take back the troth she plighted with you, and to tell you that all is forever over between you!

CAPTAIN JINKS. I won't have that! I can explain!

PROFESSOR BELLIARTI. Explain! Your signature *explains* too much already!

CAPTAIN JINKS. I don't acknowledge you or your authority! I'll see the lady herself!

PROFESSOR BELLIARTI. Not with my permission. [*Stepping in front of him.*]

CAPTAIN JINKS. *Without* it then! I tell you I won't take your word for it! *She* herself gave me her promise, and she herself must break it.

PROFESSOR BELLIARTI. I don't believe she'll ever willingly set eyes on you again!

CAPTAIN JINKS. She *must*, I tell you! It's an outrage! It's a conspiracy!

PROFESSOR BELLIARTI. There you are right! A damnable conspiracy against a sweet woman; a contemptible insult to as lovely a girl as lives. Good-by!

CAPTAIN JINKS

CAPTAIN JINKS. I won't leave this room till I've seen her.

PROFESSOR BELLIARTI. Yes, you will.

CAPTAIN JINKS. I will not!

PROFESSOR BELLIARTI. Then the police would be called in to remove you, and you would add — to what you have already done — a public scandal for Madame Trentoni on the eve of her début.

CAPTAIN JINKS. On the eve of her début? No, no! I mustn't do that— [*Quietly.*] Listen about that bet— [*Interrupted.*]

PROFESSOR BELLIARTI. Not one further word about it! The paper speaks for itself. Good-by.

CAPTAIN JINKS [*seizes the leaf and tears it angrily*]. That for your damned paper! You shall dance at our wedding yet, Papa Belliarti! [*Going to the door.*]

PROFESSOR BELLIARTI. It will be the dance Macabre then!

CAPTAIN JINKS [*turning at the door*]. Wait and see! I'm aware who's at the bottom of this and I'll find them both before the afternoon is over. And I'll make you glad to take that "blackguard" back! You don't know *me*. [*He exits.*]

PROFESSOR BELLIARTI. I wish to God we didn't.

He sinks into the arm-chair beside the table. The double doors at the back open slowly and AURELIA

CAPTAIN JINKS

steals in. She is a tearful, tragic, woe-begone-looking creature.

AURELIA. Gone?

PROFESSOR BELLIARTI. Yes.

AURELIA [*coming up behind his chair*]. Didn't you hear me drop the book a second time?

PROFESSOR BELLIARTI. No; what was that for?

AURELIA. To hint perhaps I had better see him after all, just to hear what excuse he had to make.

PROFESSOR BELLIARTI. No, no, my dear, better not.

AURELIA. Why didn't he *lie* about it? Why did he own he made it?

PROFESSOR BELLIARTI. His case was desperate! Come, you must be strong now and hold up your head.

AURELIA. I can't, I can't, Papa. My head is as heavy as my heart! [*Sitting on his lap and throwing her arms about his neck she sobs.*]—And I shan't sing to-night!—You mustn't ask me!—I—I couldn't sing a note!

PROFESSOR BELLIARTI. Not make your début to-night!

AURELIA [*her tears gone, becoming angry and a little hard*]. No! You can send word to Mapleson! You can do what you please. [*Leaving his knee, she paces up and down the room.*] I will *not* sing to-night!—Don't you know what I told you a little while ago, that I was so happy I would sing as I never sang before! Well, I was wrong. [*Beginning to cry again.*] What I should have said was—I will be so miserable, so utterly unhappy, that I'll never *sing another note!* [*She sits on the piano stool and buries her tearful face in her arms over the keys.*]

PROFESSOR BELLIARTI [*really alarmed*]. My dear child! My dear! [*Going to her.*] Where's your character? You can't give way like this. Your whole future's at stake.

AURELIA [*sobbing*]. I don't *want* any future!

Professor BELLIARTI *pulls the bell-rope.*

PROFESSOR BELLIARTI. You must think of Mapleson, too! You haven't the right to sacrifice *him.*

AURELIA. He can say I have a "cold."

PROFESSOR BELLIARTI. No one will believe it. [*Moving the chairs from the centre of the room back against the wall.*] And the public will be down on you.

AURELIA. Oh, why does n't some one invent a new kind of cold that people will believe you when you've got it.

PETER *enters in answer to the bell.*

PETER. Yes, sir.

CAPTAIN JINKS

Professor Belliarti. Help me to move this table.

Peter. Yes, sir.

They move the centre-table out of the way, and to the opposite side of the room from Aurelia.

Professor Belliarti [*aside to* Peter]. Listen! Go downstairs to the two Blackg—*gentlemen!* you will find smoking in my room, and ask them to wait a little longer. Say I may want them to apologize to Madame Trentoni before they leave the hotel.

Peter. All right, sir.

Professor Belliarti. Say nothing to any one, but watch this bell downstairs—you'll be *paid* for it—and if I pull *three* hard separate *rings*, bring the two—[*the word sticks in his throat and he has to swallow before he can speak it*] gentlemen here at once.

Peter. Yes, sir. [*Goes to the hall door.*]

Professor Belliarti [*loudly*]. And tell Mrs. Greenborough we are ready.

Peter. Yes, sir. [*Exits.*]

Aurelia [*rising*]. What? Do you think I can go through their dance with those women now?

Professor Belliarti [*putting his arm about her*]. Yes; *I ask you* to do it, dear.

CAPTAIN JINKS

AURELIA. No, no! And what for? I tell you I shan't sing to-night!

PROFESSOR BELLIARTI. Dear girl, you must! Pull yourself together, if only for *my* sake!

AURELIA. Papa, Papa! I can't. My heart is really breaking!

Professor BELLIARTI *moves the rest of the furniture out of the way, so as to leave the centre of the room free to the dancers.* AURELIA *leans against the piano.*

PROFESSOR BELLIARTI. Don't let him see it. Don't let these three blackguard men know how hardly you take it! Let your pride save you. Be a woman!

AURELIA. I *am* one, and that's why my heart is breaking.

PROFESSOR BELLIARTI. Be a *man* then, and don't let Jinks win!

Mrs. GREENBOROUGH *and the* Ballet Ladies *come volubly through the double doors. The* Ballet Ladies *are dressed in old tights, with discarded tarlatan skirts, and combing jackets; several keep on their hats, and the widow has not removed her bonnet and veil.*

MRS. GREENBOROUGH. My love, I thought you'd never send for us. Whatever in the world— [*Interrupted.*]

CAPTAIN JINKS

PROFESSOR BELLIARTI. You stop chattering, Mrs. Gee, and get to the work at the piano. What can you play?

MRS. GREENBOROUGH [*seating herself at piano*]. I know the ballet out of "Robert, the Devil."

PROFESSOR BELLIARTI [*humming a line to see if the time is right*]. That will do. [*He turns to the* Sixth Ballet Lady, *the widow, who still holds her child's hand.*] Did you *have* to bring that child?

THE SIXTH BALLET LADY. Yes, sir; I couldn't leave her 'ome, sir, but she's as good as gold — never stirs a 'air nor breathes a syllabub. [*She takes the child to the sofa and lifting her up in her two hands plumps her down into the corner hard. Here the child remains without moving or speaking.* Mrs. MAGGITT *kisses the child and then turns to* Professor BELLIARTI.] Please, sir, I wish as you'd taike me hout of the second row and put me in the front. I don't show at hall be'ind, and I'm a poor widow and my legs is hall I've got.

PROFESSOR BELLIARTI. You forget the old adage, Mrs. Maggitt, "Distance lends enchantment." Come now, ladies!

Professor BELLIARTI *gets his violin and bow ready. The other* Ballet Ladies *stand and loll about. The* First Ballet Lady *sits comfortably in a chair. The* Second Ballet Lady *sits on the arm of this chair and*

SKETCH BY PERCY ANDERSON
for *Seventh Ballet Lady*—"*Mlle. Rosalie*"

arranges the straps of her slippers. The Third Ballet Lady *leans against the wall, believing that the World is hers! The* Fourth Ballet Lady *keeps rubbing the soles of her slippers up and down on the carpet to see that it is not too slippery. The* Fifth Ballet Lady *fidgets with her dress and her waist, etc. The* Sixth Ballet Lady *practises her steps, and the* Seventh Ballet Lady *pirouettes on one toe, and throws imaginary kisses.*

THE FOURTH BALLET LADY. I wish, Miss Peddidoes, you vill nicht so push me in der waist mid your elbows so sharp!

THE FIRST BALLET LADY. If you'd keep your big feet in your own place and not keep dancing on mine, there wouldn't be any trouble.

THE FOURTH BALLET LADY. Och Himmel! I dance besser as you mit your Chinese does!

THE FIRST BALLET LADY. Sauer-kraut! [*Sticking out her tongue at her German sister artiste.*]

The latter devotee of Terpsichore responds with an even more unladylike grimace. This leads to an immediate general imbroglio among all the excitable coryphées, the seven dividing themselves into rival factions. Professor BELLIARTI, *after several ineffectual efforts to make himself heard, goes in amongst them, at no little personal risk, and, aided by Mrs.* GREENBOROUGH, *manages to separate the two prin-*

CAPTAIN JINKS

cipal somewhat draggled and highly flushed contestants.

PROFESSOR BELLIARTI [*striking his violin with his bow*]. Attention, ladies, please! [*There is a general movement; those sitting rise.*] Let us rehearse the Pas de Rose in the first act. [*He goes to* AURELIA.] Make an effort, dearie. Speak to them. Tell them what you want.

AURELIA. No! You tell them. I can't, I can't!

The Ballet Ladies *go to a large bundle of artificial roses placed on a table in the corner and each takes one.* Miss PETTITOES *snatches her flower from* Miss HOCHSPITZ's *hand. There is an awful moment, but the widow pours oil on the waters, and quiet is preserved.*

PROFESSOR BELLIARTI. An elaborate ballet in this opera has not been done in America before, and we want it to be perfect.

The Ballet Ladies *take their positions.* AURELIA *starts to leave the room.* Professor BELLIARTI *stops her.*

AURELIA. Let me go to my room.

PROFESSOR BELLIARTI. No, dearie, please, *please* stay. Don't let these women see you are in trouble. Are you ready, Mrs. Gee?

MRS. GREENBOROUGH. Good gracious, I've been— [*Interrupted.*]

CAPTAIN JINKS

Professor Belliarti. Very good! Ready, please! [*He and* Mrs. Greenborough *begin playing.*] One, two, three, etc., *ad lib.* [*The* Ballet Ladies *begin their dance*, Professor Belliarti *leading and directing them, dancing with them, showing them, correcting them; after a minute he speaks aside to* Aurelia.] Try to watch them, dear. [*He continues with the dance, but again, a few minutes later, he stops and speaks to her, the ballet always continuing without him.*] Be brave, little girl! You have your life before you, and if the fellow's worthless, why let him spoil it?

Aurelia. That's perfectly true, only—

Professor Belliarti. Keep only one idea now in your mind—*your appearance to-night.*

Aurelia. I'll try, I'll try!

Professor Belliarti. That's my brave girl. Look at that silly creature! [*Directing her attention to one of the* Ballet Ladies, *he tries to excite her interest in the dancers.*] They're doing very badly. What do you think?

Aurelia [*watching them*]. Oh, atrocious! They are n't ballet girls, they're tenpins!

The first movement of the ballet is finished.

Professor Belliarti [*urging her*]. Show them! That's the only way they will learn.

CAPTAIN JINKS

AURELIA. No, I can't, not now. Who dances the solo?

PROFESSOR BELLIARTI [*to the* Ballet Ladies]. The *pas seul*, please! [*All but the* Fourth *and* First Ballet Ladies *retire and take seats. The* Fourth Ballet Lady *comes forward.*] No, no, Miss Hochspitz, not the next figure; the *pas seul*, Miss Pettitoes!

THE FIRST BALLET LADY [*laughs*]. Hochspitz doing a solo! Ha, ha! A cabbage by any other name would smell as sweet! [*She gracefully kicks a satirical kiss to her with her right foot.*] "Blue Danube," please.

THE THIRD BALLET LADY [*to the* First Ballet Lady]. Ssh! Ssh!

PROFESSOR BELLIARTI [*who has taken the* First Ballet Lady *to one side*]. Dance badly, *very badly!*

THE FIRST BALLET LADY [*insulted*]. Badly?

PROFESSOR BELLIARTI. Yes, it will be all right. I have a reason.

The First Ballet Lady *dances not very well.* Professor BELLIARTI *watches* AURELIA, *who remains indifferent.*

PROFESSOR BELLIARTI [*to the* First Ballet Lady]. That isn't bad enough — dance worse!

THE FIRST BALLET LADY [*angry*]. I *can't!*

PROFESSOR BELLIARTI. Try! —

CAPTAIN JINKS

THE FIRST BALLET LADY [*still dancing*]. I'm afraid I'll lose my job.

PROFESSOR BELLIARTI. You will if you don't do as I ask.

THE FIRST BALLET LADY [*very angry*]. Oh! All right! [*She dances very badly.*]

PROFESSOR BELLIARTI [*to* AURELIA]. Now, do watch, dear.

AURELIA [*noticing*]. But that girl's awful!

PROFESSOR BELLIARTI [*to* AURELIA]. Show her.

AURELIA. No. [*But she rises and pins up one side of her dress.*]

PROFESSOR BELLIARTI [*to the* First Ballet Lady]. Go on! *worse!!*

He goes to the bell-rope and pulls three distinct times. The First Ballet Lady *dances a pas seul vilely.*

AURELIA [*excitedly*]. She's wrong! — *she's all wrong!!* [*Pinning up the other side of her dress.*]

PROFESSOR BELLIARTI [*to the* First Ballet Lady]. You're wrong again! [*The music stops.*]

THE FIRST BALLET LADY. Wrong!

PROFESSOR BELLIARTI. Show her, dear, show her!—

AURELIA. It's simple as daylight! Give me a rose! [*Seizing her rose from* Miss PETTITOES.]

CAPTAIN JINKS

PROFESSOR BELLIARTI. That's right! [*Striking up on his violin.*] Now watch Madame Trentoni. [Mrs. GREENBOROUGH *begins playing again.*]

AURELIA [*dancing*]. One—two—three—

PROFESSOR BELLIARTI [*always playing*]. Ah, do you see the difference, Miss Pettitoes?

AURELIA [*dancing*]. Not as if you were made of wood! Ah, Papa, I wish I were! [*Stopping dancing as if she couldn't do it.*]

PROFESSOR BELLIARTI. Careful!

PETER *enters, showing in* GUSSIE *and* CHARLIE.

PETER. Mr. La Martine, Mr. Van Vorkenburg! [*The music stops again.*]

AURELIA [*astonished*]. What?

PROFESSOR BELLIARTI [*to* AURELIA]. Your pride!

CHARLIE [*coming forward*]. We have come, Madame Trentoni, to apologize.

AURELIA. Apologize? I won't listen to you!

GUSSIE. We regret very much to have made you suffer.

AURELIA. Suffer! *I suffer?* [*Laughing.*] What for? You surely don't suppose I take this matter of Captain Jinks seriously? [*Laughing a little hysterically.*] I, who have the *world* at my feet! Suffer? [*With increased excitement.*] Excuse me, gentlemen,

but I can't have my rehearsal interrupted. Continue, Mrs. Gee. Now, ladies, please watch me! [*Mrs. Greenborough plays. Aurelia dances with abandon.*] Smile and look happy! [*She does so pathetically and then dances on with ever increasing excitement.*] Dance as if you *loved* it! as if it *meant* something! Put your *whole heart* into it! if you're so lucky as to have one! [*Executing a difficult movement. All clap their hands, delighted at her dancing. Charlie and Gussie stand by somewhat crestfallen, and look questioningly at each other. They applaud, too, and then take advantage of the moment to slip out unnoticed.*] *Dance!!* Don't *walk! Dance*—as if you were *mad!* Dance! Never mind if you break your neck—there are worse things to break! *Dance!! Dance!!!* [*The strain of music finishes and she stops suddenly, throwing away her rose.*] Papa, *I will sing*, after all! I'll sing to every woman's heart in that house, and if ever I succeed in my life, *I'll win tonight!*

Professor Belliarti. Bravo! Bravo!

Aurelia *turns and sees* La Martine *and* Van Vorkenburg *are gone, and in a revulsion of feeling collapses in her old foster-father's arms, sobbing out pitifully,* "*Oh, no, I can't do it, I can't do it,*" *as the curtain falls.*

THE END OF ACT II

THE THIRD ACT

THE THIRD ACT

MIDNIGHT OF THE SAME DAY—*The same room as in the previous act,* Madame TRENTONI's *parlor in the Brevoort House. The stage is lighted by chandelier with gas-jets.*

PETER [*entering with his arms full of flowers*]. Come on in!

MARY *stands at the back with her arms also full of floral emblems,—a large windmill, baskets, a ship, and small bouquets.*

MARY [*who speaks with a decided English cockney accent*]. Oh my! Was n't it grand! [*Places the windmill of pink and white dried daisies on the piano.*] I could 'ear 'em shouting way hup in the dressing-room!

PETER [*who is very hoarse*]. I bet they heard the gallery way over to Broadway! *I* led the gallery! and gee! I guess I broke my voice. [*Deposits his flowers about.*]

MARY [*as she arranges*]. Did you see General Grant?

CAPTAIN JINKS

PETER. *Did* I? Did n't you hear us give three cheers when he come in! [*Very huskily.*] Hip! hip! hooray! and Sam Tilden — he's another big man — he got it just as good!

There is a knock at the hall door.

MARY. Come in!

She hangs a wreath of pansies on a door-knob and meets one of the hotel Servants, *who enters laden down with more floral emblems, — small baskets with huge handles, pillows with "Welcome" on them, etc.* MARY *relieves him of his burden and he exits.* PETER *and* MARY *arrange the new pieces around the room.*

PETER. She got piles of flowers, did n't she?

MARY. Oh, this ain't harlf!

PETER [*sitting at the piano and picking out "Captain Jinks" with one hand while he talks*]. When 's she coming home?

MARY [*very busy*]. Soon as she can shake off her the newspaper gentlemen, and a 'eap of people.

PETER. She must have been tickled to death with the send-off we give her!

MARY [*loading down the mantel*]. No, something 's the matter with her; you 'd 'ave thought they was all a 'issing instead of shouting, she looked that mournful, and heven took hon to crying once.

CAPTAIN JINKS

PETER. Aw, go West! you don't know what you're talking about! When I went behind after the show, she was grinning fit to kill, telling them newspaper gents that it was the finest gang of folks she'd ever sung afore!

MARY. Yes, she told me when she was chainging hafter the third hact that they was *dears* hin front and that she just loved them, and was doing her very best.

PETER. Say, who do you think was there! I seen her down in the balcony and crying fit to bust herself all through the last ack! The old lady whot was here this afternoon! [*He suddenly shouts.*] Look out! [*As* MARY *is about to put a large horseshoe of red immortelles with a big "Pete" in white immortelles on it, off at one side of the room in an inconspicuous place.*] What yer doing with my hor'shoe? [*Taking it from her.*] It took my first month's wages in advance to get that! [*He places it proudly on the centre-table and stands off and looks at it.*] Ain't it a dream! Don't it look just like her!

MARY. Oh, lovely! Is heverything ready for the supper? [*Going towards the double doors at the back, but* PETER *gets there before her and stops her.*]

PETER. Here, you can't go in! The hotel folks don't want any one in there afore her. It's all done up with regular Fourth of July decorations.

CAPTAIN JINKS

MARY. Well, there's more helegant hemblems downstairs and the 'all gentleman don't seem to be bringing 'em hup. I fancy I'd better get 'em. [*And she goes out.*]

PETER *watches that she is surely gone, and then opening one of the big double doors, whistles softly through his fingers and waits a second.* Captain JINKS *comes in eagerly.*

CAPTAIN JINKS. Is it safe?

PETER. Yes, for a minute; she's gone after more flower pieces. Are them yourn? [*Pointing to some bouquets and baskets grouped together.*]

CAPTAIN JINKS. Yes. [*Examining them. He adds to himself in an undertone:*] And not one of my notes removed! But I saw her pick up the white camellia. She must have read that!

PETER. Mary says she did n't pay no attention to none of her flowers, and even piped her eyes some!

CAPTAIN JINKS. Cried! My dear Peter, that's a good sign! [*Taking out a bundle of small notes from his pocket.*] If only she loves me, I'm sure I can make it all right. Come along now, quick, put one of these notes on all the other flowers. [*They begin quickly pinning on notes to all the bouquets, baskets, etc.*]

PETER. I don't know as I ought to be helping

you this way. After all, I've *only got your word for* it that you didn't really mean to try and do Madame Trentoni out of her money.

CAPTAIN JINKS. Yes, but what did I tell you my word would be worth to you?

PETER. A couple o' fivers! but it's taking fearful risks, and I ain't got her *happiness* fer sale, I want yer to understand that. But say, you didn't send her all these, here's somebody else's card.

CAPTAIN JINKS. That's all right. [*Crossing to the flowers on the piano.*] Leave it on, but put mine too. I want one of my notes on every single thing here!

PETER [*pinning the notes about*]. Gee! You're a great writer, ain't you? Have you written all them different?

CAPTAIN JINKS. No, they're all alike. [*Coming to centre-table he starts to pin a note on* PETER's *horse-shoe.*]

PETER. Here! No, you don't! Look out! Not on that one! That's *mine!* I ain't goin' to hev no interference with *mine!*

CAPTAIN JINKS. Oh, come on, yours might be the only one she looked at! Let me put on my note, and I'll pay for the horseshoe.

PETER. But you won't pretend *you sent it?* Honest Injun?

CAPTAIN JINKS

CAPTAIN JINKS. Honest!

PETER. All right, anything to oblige a friend; it'll be five dollars, please.

MARY'S *voice is heard outside, saying: "This way. Come straight along. Oh! I dropped a bouquet; beg pardon."* PETER *and* Captain JINKS *have stopped and* Captain JINKS *goes to the double doors quickly.*

CAPTAIN JINKS. Don't forget, you're to manage somehow that I get an interview with Mrs. Greenborough. No interview—no pay.

PETER. That's all right! You just trust yourself to little brother.

CAPTAIN JINKS [*thrusting a handful of notes into* PETER'S *hands*]. Try and get those on the rest of the flowers. [*He exits.*]

PETER [*calling after him*]. Quick! Hide in the further room, they may go in this one.

He shuts the doors as MARY *enters loaded down with more flowers, and followed by* Mrs. STONINGTON *and* Miss MERRIAM, *without their hats and with a flower in their hair, the waist of* Mrs. STONINGTON'S *dress turned in a trifle at the neck.*

MARY. Won't you sit down, please? The hother guests will suttingly be 'ere soon.

MARY *places about the flowers she has just brought up.* PETER *continues pinning on the notes.*

CAPTAIN JINKS

Mrs. Stonington. It was very kind of Madame Trentoni to ask us to supper on such an occasion. She is the greatest singer I've ever heard. [*Turns to* Miss Merriam *and repeats with most careful enunciation.*] *An elegant singer!*

Miss Merriam *smiles and nods, and makes a few rapid motions with her fingers.*

Mrs. Stonington. Oh, yes, very hot! Where we sat—we were in the back row, gallery; we found it very difficult to get seats. [Mary *is about to pass her with a small basket of flowers with a very high handle on which is perched a stuffed pigeon with outstretched wings.* Mrs. Stonington *stops* Mary.] The dove! [*She examines the card, which is tied on with a blue ribbon, and then nods to* Miss Merriam.] Yes, *our* emblem!

Mary. I never 'eard madam sing Traiviatter so magnificent before! [*She crosses to the piano with the emblem.*]

Miss Merriam *motions again a few words to* Mrs. Stonington.

Mrs. Stonington. *No, indeed!* I didn't see a single bad thing in it! [Miss Merriam *motions again.*] No, sir, not a blessed thing! I agree with you to an iota; I think it's a sweetly pretty opera! [Miss Merriam *makes a few more rapid passes.*] Exactly! Neither did I understand what it was about, but nobody has any need to; it's enough to hear her voice and see her clothes! [Miss MERRIAM *motions.*] My dear, you never spoke a truer word! You can find a bad meaning in most everything in this world if you want to, and only try hard enough.

MRS. GREENBOROUGH [*calls outside in the hall*]. Mary!

MARY. Yes, madam. [*Going to the hall door she opens it.*]

MRS. STONINGTON. Here's dear Mrs. Greenborough! and she does look sweetly pretty to-night!

Mrs. GREENBOROUGH *enters, both arms full of floral trophies.*

MRS. GREENBOROUGH. What an elegant triumph, Mary! Did you *ever* in all the days you've been with Madame Trentoni— [*Interrupted.*]

MARY. No, indeed, ma'am. [*Helping* Mrs. GREENBOROUGH *relieve herself of the flowers.*] I *never* 'eard such a grand reception!

PETER [*who is pinning notes on bouquets in a corner*]. Bet your life! you could n't beat our gallery! [*He begins to pin* Captain JINKS' *notes to the flowers* Mrs. GREENBOROUGH *has just brought in.*]

MRS. STONINGTON. Good evening, Mrs. Greenborough.

MRS. GREENBOROUGH [*turning*]. Oh! You are

here, my dears; excuse me, I didn't see you! [*Kissing them both.*] Well, what do you think? Did you ever in your life! Wasn't I right or did I— [*Interrupted.*]

MRS. STONINGTON. No siree, you didn't exaggerate one bit! We are going to make a report to the League that her voice is superb.

Miss MERRIAM *tugs at her elbow.* Mrs. STONINGTON *turns.* Miss MERRIAM *makes a few motions.*

MRS. STONINGTON [*to* Miss MERRIAM]. Yes, dear. [*To* Mrs. GREENBOROUGH.] We're going to add to our report that *any one* can go, because no one understands what it's about unless they have an evil mind.

MRS. GREENBOROUGH. Oh, my darlings, I'm so glad you think so; you remember what I told you, what I always said was— [*Interrupted.*]

MRS. STONINGTON. Yes, indeed, we've been saying it over to ourselves! And do tell me if I've got the neck of my basque too low? I've turned in *three* buttons! I wanted to be real dressy, but I don't want to catch cold. I wouldn't let Miss Merriam turn hers in, she's so delicate! I told her she'd look very stylish in her black silk if she'd put on that pretty bib of hers.

MRS. GREENBOROUGH. You both look very fetching, but I must ask you to come into another room to wait, if you don't mind. Aurelia sent me home first to see that the guests did n't assemble here.— We 've taken a little parlor on the other side of the banquet room. She 's all upset, poor child, unstrung! Come this way. [*Leading them to the double doors.* PETER *gets there first and takes* Mrs. GREENBOROUGH's *arm and whispers into her ear.*]

Mrs. STONINGTON *and* Miss MERRIAM *are trying to read the cards on the different bouquets, etc.*

MRS. GREENBOROUGH [*surprised at what* PETER *tells her*]. What! [PETER *nods his head violently.*] You little scamp! You ought to be spanked, and I 'd like to do it.

PETER. Oh, would you! I guess you 'd have your hands full! Let Miss Mary take them through the other way. [*Motioning to the hall door.*]

Mrs. GREENBOROUGH *gives* PETER *a speaking look and then turns.*

MRS. GREENBOROUGH. Ladies—Mary will show you into the room through the hall. I will join you presently.

MARY *goes to the door.* Miss MERRIAM *starts quickly to follow her.*

MRS. STONINGTON. Sophie! Sophie! [Miss MERRIAM *of course does not hear her and goes on.* Mrs. STONINGTON *runs after her and catches her at the door. She motions to her to wait.* Mrs. STONINGTON *then goes to* Mrs. GREENBOROUGH *and whispers to her questioningly.*]

MRS. GREENBOROUGH. I'll ask her!

MRS. STONINGTON. And do you think she *will?*

MRS. GREENBOROUGH. Yes, she's willing to do just *anything* for friends of mine, no matter *what* it is!

MRS. STONINGTON [*hurries to* Miss MERRIAM *and says delightedly with very careful enunciation*]. She thinks we *can* kiss her.

Miss MERRIAM *claps her hands with joy, her face wreathed in smiles, as she and* Mrs. STONINGTON *follow* MARY *out into the hall.*

MRS. GREENBOROUGH [*turning upon* PETER]. You naughty little boy, you! Why did you let Captain Jinks in there?

PETER. 'Cause he has my sympathies. You don't know all, but *I* do. He went to jail for her sake, and no hero ever done better 'n that fur his girl, not even in "The Fireside Companion"!

MRS. GREENBOROUGH. You're out of your head!

PETER. No, I ain't. [*Opening one of the double doors he whistles.*] Wait and see!

Captain JINKS *comes in.*

CAPTAIN JINKS

Mrs. Greenborough. Well, sir, I must say— [*Interrupted.*]

Captain Jinks. Don't! Don't say it! We haven't much time! Persuade Madame Trentoni to see me.

Mrs. Greenborough. Papa Belliarti has told me what you did— [*Interrupted.*]

Captain Jinks. If I could see her I could explain.

Mrs. Greenborough. I don't think explaining could do us much good!

Captain Jinks. Yes, it would, if she loves me.

Mrs. Greenborough. *Loves you? Now!* After that scandalous wager?

Captain Jinks. Well, then, if she *ever* loved me, if she *ever* loved me—I'm sure I can persuade her.

Mrs. Greenborough. I don't mind telling you, young man, that she *did* love you, that's the blessed truth! If you could have heard her talk in her sleep as *I* have! Why, only the other afternoon— [*Interrupted.*]

Captain Jinks. She *did* love me?

Mrs. Greenborough. Yes, she did. I don't see any harm in telling that— [*Interrupted.*]

Captain Jinks [*suddenly in outburst of joy hugs* Mrs. Greenborough *and kisses her*]. God bless you, Mrs. Gee! God bless you for that!

SKETCH BY PERCY ANDERSON
for *Mrs. Greenborough*

CAPTAIN JINKS

PETER *half enters hurriedly.*

PETER. Psst! [*He sees them embracing.*] Hully Gee! [*They separate.*] Say, *which one* is it you're after? [*Laughing.*]

CAPTAIN JINKS [*laughing*]. Shut up, Peter!

PETER. Well, you'd better get—she's coming.

MRS. GREENBOROUGH. Oh, *do* go! She's in an awful hysterical state. No, not that way!

CAPTAIN JINKS [*at the double doors*]. Yes, I shall wait here till you bring me word she *will* see me. She *must* see me! Yes, to-night!

MRS. GREENBOROUGH. *No; to-morrow!*

CAPTAIN JINKS. NO; TO-NIGHT! [*He exits.*]

MRS. GREENBOROUGH [*to* PETER]. Take him through into the parlor where the other guests are assembling; don't let him stay in there. [*Pushing* PETER *out after* Captain JINKS.] O dear me, sirs, what am I to do?

Professor BELLIARTI *comes in, and* AURELIA *follows. She is gowned in a billowy mass of white tarlatan, showered over with pink rosebuds, and emphasized here and there with bright green ribbon. Her bustle and train crowd the furniture in the room. A wreath of pink rosebuds is on her head. She carries a cloak and a white lace scarf in her hands and a bouquet; she throws them away from her any-*

where. Mrs. GREENBOROUGH *runs after her and picks them up.*

PROFESSOR BELLIARTI. For just five minutes, Aurelia, come, please!

AURELIA [*with determination*]. No, Papa, I cannot.

PROFESSOR BELLIARTI [*to* Mrs. GREENBOROUGH]. I want her to be present at her supper.

AURELIA. You can make any excuse for me you like!

PROFESSOR BELLIARTI. But—my dear child—

AURELIA. I mean it, Papa. I've sung to-night for your sake more than anything else, but I can't do anything more, and it's the last time I'll do that.

MRS. GREENBOROUGH. Aurelia! When you never had so great a triumph!

AURELIA. Triumph? Triumph? Over a few people!

PROFESSOR BELLIARTI. *Few* people! Many *hundreds!*

AURELIA. *Hundreds* then! and what do I care? The only triumph I want is denied me, the *triumph of love!* Oh, Papa, you can't understand how I feel, —you're only a *man!* You say the people to-night stood up and shouted themselves hoarse! Did they? I heard nothing but the beating of my poor heart. You say I have been deluged with gifts of flowers, but the only gift I want is missing—one man's honest love! *with that*, to-night *would have been* a triumph! I would have given him my success as my first gift, but without his love it all means nothing. I don't want success! I don't want anything—

MRS. GREENBOROUGH. Not even any supper?

AURELIA. No, no, ask them to excuse me. [*She sinks on the piano stool and buries her face in her arms and cries. A brass band strikes up loudly outside the window, "Hail! the Conquering Hero Comes," and at the same moment* PETER *rushes in.*]

PETER. Hurrah! There's a big band come to serenade Madame Trentoni. You must go to the window. [*He runs out.*]

Professor BELLIARTI *opens a window. Loud cries come from the outside—"Trentoni!" "Trentoni!"*

MRS. GREENBOROUGH [*in great excitement*]. Oh! isn't it beautiful!

PROFESSOR BELLIARTI [*to* AURELIA]. Come, dear. Come and bow to them.

AURELIA [*sobbing*]. I can't! I can't!

PROFESSOR BELLIARTI. You must! It will anger them.

MRS. GREENBOROUGH. O goodness! you mustn't do that, Aurelia!

PROFESSOR BELLIARTI. Nurse your success; it will mean everything.

AURELIA. No.

Louder cries again of "Aurelia!" "Aurelia!" and "Trentoni!" and wilder shouts still outside. PETER *again runs in.*

PETER. Quick, *please!* Bow at the window! They're beginning to get mad! [*Again he runs out shouting.*]

PROFESSOR BELLIARTI. Come! Come to the window!

A few "baas" and hisses are heard; then the shouts and the band stop.

AURELIA. No! No!

PROFESSOR BELLIARTI. Mrs. Gee! Quick, put Aurelia's scarf on your head! [*She does so.*] You must take her place.

MRS. GREENBOROUGH. But do you think we look anything alike?

PROFESSOR BELLIARTI. Never mind, it's dark, they can't distinguish anything! Come on! [*Taking her to the window.*] Bow to them and wave! [*She does so.*] That's it! Again!

Great shouts and hurrahs. Cries of "Trentoni forever!" "God bless you, Aurelia!" etc. The band plays "The Star-Spangled Banner." AURELIA *begins to listen and show some interest.*

PROFESSOR BELLIARTI. Throw them kisses.

CAPTAIN JINKS

Mrs. GREENBOROUGH *does so. Increased shouts and cries of* "*Speech!*" "*Speech!*"

MRS. GREENBOROUGH [*laughing excitedly*]. O good gracious! what'll I do now?

PROFESSOR BELLIARTI. Speak! Say something!

AURELIA [*quickly*]. No! Come away from the window—I'll speak to them. [Mrs. GREENBOROUGH *has come away. When she leaves the window the clamor outside hushes disappointedly.* AURELIA *takes the lace scarf and goes to the window, really moved, and speaks.*] How good of them! This morning how I should have loved this! [*She reaches the window, and the applause and shouts double, with louder cries of* "*Speech,*" *and the band stops.*] Thank you! [*Hurrahs and bravos very loud outside.*] Thank you all! [*More shouts and greater applause.*] Thank you! [*She throws kisses with both hands, and adds in an excited outburst:*] You're *darlings*, every one of you! [*Tremendous cheers as she leaves the window, and the brass band strikes up* "*Champagne Charlie.*" *It dies away with the shouts of the crowd outside, as they gradually disperse.* AURELIA *has gone from the window to the piano and takes up a note there on the flowers. She reads it.*] "I must see you! There has been a terrible mistake. If you ever loved me give me an interview."

PROFESSOR BELLIARTI [*who has followed her,*

CAPTAIN JINKS

speaks softly over her shoulder]. Don't trust him.

AURELIA *continues reading the other notes and shows on her face her surprise at finding them all the same.*

MRS. GREENBOROUGH. Papa, you go to our guests, and I'll speak to Aurelia.

PROFESSOR BELLIARTI. No, *you* go; I have something to say to her.

AURELIA [*still reads the notes*]. I must see you! There is a terrible mistake! If ever you loved me —

Mrs. GREENBOROUGH *goes out through the double doors.* PETER *comes in after knocking.*

PETER. Say! General Sherman's just come, and they all want to know where Madame Trentoni is.

PROFESSOR BELLIARTI. Mrs. Greenborough has gone to them.

PETER. Hurry up! They're getting mad, and one of them ballet girls — the widder — is hooking oranges from off the table. She says it's for the kid! [*He exits.*]

AURELIA. But these notes are all the same! [*Looking quickly at another.*] The same! —

PROFESSOR BELLIARTI [*reading one on the centre-table*]. The same! Here, dear, don't read them. [*Gathering several unread notes into his hands and crushing them.*]

CAPTAIN JINKS

AURELIA. No! No! Papa! [*Taking them out of his hands.*] Be careful! I *want* to *read* them—every one!

A knock is heard on the hall door.

PROFESSOR BELLIARTI. Come in.

AURELIA. Please! I don't want to see any one.

The Fourth Ballet Lady—Miss HOCHSPITZ—*enters, followed by all the other* Ballet Ladies, *who group themselves in a semicircle behind her.*

THE FOURTH BALLET LADY. Pardong! I haf com mit ein kleine message from der ballet laties. [*With a curtsey.*]

PROFESSOR BELLIARTI. Madame Trentoni is very ill. Worn out with the excitement of her début.

THE FOURTH BALLET LADY. Yah! Das is vat de old woman dold us, und ve vas all so traublich. I rebresend de 'ole ballet laties ven I com und says dat ve all gif to Madame Drendoni our loaf und say vat she vas vunderschone, und der pest singer vat ve has effer tanced mit! [*Curtsies and kisses* AURELIA'S *hand.*]

All the Ballet Ladies *clap their hands and cry* "*Hear! Hear!*"

AURELIA. Thank you very much, and all the ladies! I'm sure you all danced very well, too.

THE FOURTH BALLET LADY. Ve haf madt besser

mit our feets ven you haf made so goot mit your mouth!

AURELIA. Thank you again, and I hope you will all enjoy your supper.

THE FOURTH BALLET LADY. Ve vill *eat [the widow here inadvertently claps]*, aber not so much ven you vas nicht mit der party. Dis wreat vas made py our own hands just now mit schnips from oud of our own bouquets [*giving wreath*] — vat vas gif us py our *sveethearts!*

AURELIA. Thank you.

THE FOURTH BALLET LADY. Gude nacht! Ve vill all pet our toes you vas de greadest success effer vas! *Gude nacht!*

They all curtsey and turn to go out through the double doors at the back. As they exit PETTITOES *and* HOCHSPITZ *embrace, in an excess of good feeling.*

PROFESSOR BELLIARTI. Good night. [*Closing the door behind them.*]

AURELIA. You go to the supper, too, dear Papa.

PROFESSOR BELLIARTI. No, dearie, I can't leave you.

A knock on the hall door.

AURELIA [*again bright and hopeful*]. Maybe that's he. Come in.

PETER *enters.*

CAPTAIN JINKS

PETER. This came for you this evening from the Everett House. [*Giving* AURELIA *an envelope.*]

AURELIA. Thank you.

PETER [*to* Professor BELLIARTI]. Did you see my hor'shoe? I tell yer! [*He exits haughtily.*]

PROFESSOR BELLIARTI. What is that?

AURELIA. Two tickets for the vessel that sails to-morrow for Liverpool.

PROFESSOR BELLIARTI. Where did you get them?

AURELIA. I sent for them between the acts,—for Mary and me.

PROFESSOR BELLIARTI [*sternly*]. *Give* me those tickets!

AURELIA. No!

PROFESSOR BELLIARTI [*determined*]. I've never coerced you in your life. Have I, dear?

AURELIA [*as determined*]. No, and I have never disobeyed you, have I?

PROFESSOR BELLIARTI. No, and you will not go away to-morrow.

AURELIA. This time if *you* coerce, *I* disobey.

PROFESSOR BELLIARTI. You *can't* go away! What about Mr. Mapleson?

AURELIA. He can send for Adelina Patti! She made a furore here a year or so ago.

CAPTAIN JINKS

Professor Belliarti. Adelina Patti is n't *you*.

Aurelia. Oh, well, she's as young as I, and a better singer—if the truth's told.

Professor Belliarti. But your contract?

Aurelia. Oh, *hang* my contract!

Professor Belliarti. We can't! It'll hang us! Give me those tickets.

Aurelia [*holding them up in front of his face*]. In exchange for Captain Jinks—for nothing else.

Professor Belliarti. Won't you realize he is unworthy of you?

Aurelia. *He* said so, and I would n't believe it, and I shan't believe it when *you* say so, either.

Professor Belliarti. Well, we'll go to supper now—we'll talk it over later.

Aurelia. No, I must pack, with Mary; we have n't much time.

Professor Belliarti. No; come with me now—you *must*.

Aurelia. I *won't!* There! [*Taking off one of her long curls that hang from the back of her waterfall.*] And there! [*Taking off the other curl and placing both upon the piano.*] *Now* will you believe me? [*A knock on the hall door.*] Oh! perhaps that's *he!* Wait a minute, Papa! don't say "come in" yet!

CAPTAIN JINKS

[*And she quickly puts back both curls.*] Now!—come in! [*Pathetically.*]

The Policeman, *remembered in Act I, enters with much assurance.*

THE POLICEMAN. Beg pardon, ma'am, but is Captain Jinks here?

AURELIA [*echoes, surprised*]. Captain Jinks!

PROFESSOR BELLIARTI. Certainly not!

THE POLICEMAN. Well, he was seen coming into the hotel not so long since, and I thought maybe as he was one of the invites at your party—

PROFESSOR BELLIARTI. I can assure you that the apartment of Madame Trentoni is the last place you would find Captain Jinks—that gentleman is no longer our friend.

THE POLICEMAN. Don't say! Well, he's skipped his bail this afternoon which your Mr. Mapleson put up for him, and he's wanted by the police.

AURELIA [*faintly, in astonishment and distress*]. The police?—

PROFESSOR BELLIARTI. Why did Mr. Mapleson go bail for him?

THE POLICEMAN. Give it up! Echo answers why!

PROFESSOR BELLIARTI. I mean—what's he done? Why—

CAPTAIN JINKS

AURELIA [*stops* Professor BELLIARTI]. Papa! That's not our affair. We have no interest in Captain Jinks' *misdeeds!* [*She turns to the* Policeman.] Good night, sir.

THE POLICEMAN [*going, slightly embarrassed*]. Good night, ma'am. [*He comes back, becoming more and more embarrassed, however.*] Beg pardon, ma'am, I was in the lobby of the Academy to-night, trying to keep the aisles free, and had to give it up as a bad job! But even with the doors shut I could hear you — some of them high notes of yourn came clean through the wood! It was *grand!* They fairly put my teeth on edge! The best I ever heard!

AURELIA [*half smiling*]. Thank you. [*Shakes his hand, which makes him very proud.*]

THE POLICEMAN. Thank you. Good night, ma'am — good night, sir! [*Bows, and exits.*]

AURELIA *and* Professor BELLIARTI *look at each other a second in silence.*

PROFESSOR BELLIARTI. Now you understand Mapleson's knowledge — and you *have* had an escape, my dear.

AURELIA. I don't believe — not even yet. I don't *want* to escape!

Mrs. GREENBOROUGH *returns.*

MRS. GREENBOROUGH. Everybody's arrived, dear

heart, so I thought it best for us to come into the supper room and begin. I hope I haven't gone and— [*Interrupted.*]

Professor Belliarti. You haven't. You did quite right, Mrs. Gee!

Mrs. Greenborough. Aurelia *won't* come?

Professor Belliarti. No. But I'll start things going.

They go to the double doors and Mrs. Greenborough *exits.* Professor Belliarti, *about to follow, changes his mind, and closing the door, goes back to* Aurelia. *As* Mrs. Greenborough *exits the guests in the back room begin to sing "Auld Lang Syne," which is heard more faintly when the door is closed.* Aurelia *sits on the piano stool, her head and arms on the piano.*

Professor Belliarti [*leans over her, and speaks softly*]. Shall I make a little speech for you, dearie, and say you thank them all, and want them to have a happy evening?

Aurelia, *who cannot speak because of her tears, lifts her head and nods "Yes." Professor* Belliarti *goes into the back room and the singing is louder as the door opens—till it is shut.* Aurelia, *when she realizes she is alone, takes from the bosom of her dress a white camellia to which is attached a note, which she reads aloud in a pathetic little voice, half crying all through and breaking down entirely at the end.*

AURELIA. "I must see you—there is a terrible mistake—if you ever loved me, give me an interview—" [*She cries softly, leaning her head and arms on the piano. She then rises, deliberately, and pulls the bell-cord.*] I'll see him myself. He hasn't had any chance to explain and I'll give it to him—but I won't make it easy!

PETER *enters in answer to the bell.*

PETER. Yes, ma'am?

AURELIA. Peter, do you want to do me a favor?

PETER. Oh! bet your life.

AURELIA. I'll pay you well.

PETER. No, you *won't!* Not from *you.* Not *this* boy!

AURELIA. I'm afraid it'll be hard for you, but do you think you *could* find Captain Jinks *somewhere* to-night, and bring him here—without telling any one?

PETER [*secretly amused*]. Well—I might *try*—if you don't mind waiting! Of course, if he's way over to Brooklyn—

AURELIA. I *won't* mind waiting if you'll only *find* him!

CAPTAIN JINKS

PETER. I guess I'll tell you the truth! [*Delighted.*] He's right *here!*

AURELIA. *Here?*

PETER. Yes, ma'am! He's been in this room. He and I put all them notes on!

AURELIA. You did! You brought him here? You're a dear boy! [*She kisses his cheek.* PETER, *overcome with joy, pride, and emotion, holds his hand to his cheek.*]

PETER. *O! Gee!* Thank you! I'll *never wash* that spot!

AURELIA. Now listen! Don't let Captain Jinks know I sent you for him! Pretend I don't know he's here and just send him in.

PETER. It won't take much *sending.* It's been all I could do to keep him out! [*He exits.*]

AURELIA. Of course he can explain! I knew it, and he's only been waiting for his chance. [*Tears up the steamer tickets.*] But he's got to work for it; he must be punished a little for—something or other! I'm sure I must look a fright, after all I've gone through. [*Standing on the sofa she looks at herself in the glass over the mantel.*] I'll just put a little dab of powder on— [*She hurries out through the door to her bedroom as* PETER *shows in* Captain JINKS.]

CAPTAIN JINKS

CAPTAIN JINKS. She's not here!

PETER. Oh, I guess she has gone to her room to prink up a little!

CAPTAIN JINKS. For her guests at supper?

PETER. No, she won't join them—it's for *you*.

CAPTAIN JINKS. But she doesn't expect to see me, does she?

PETER. Look here, all's fair in love and war! Guess I'll tell you the truth—*she* sent me after you!

CAPTAIN JINKS [*not daring to believe his ears*]. What!

PETER [*laughing*]. She told me to try hard to find you; but don't tell—she said to keep "mum"!

CAPTAIN JINKS. Peter, you're an ideal boy—here's a dollar for you! [*Gives him a bill.*]

PETER. Thank you! [*Exits.*]

The guests are heard through the double doors singing "Champagne Charlie." AURELIA *reënters.*

AURELIA [*stopping short in an only partially successful effort to simulate surprise*]. Captain Jinks!

CAPTAIN JINKS. Madame!

AURELIA. How dared you come here? Had you sent your card I should have refused to see you! [*With great but not altogether convincing hauteur.*]

CAPTAIN JINKS

CAPTAIN JINKS. And had you sent for me I should have refused to come!

AURELIA. *I send* for you! Impossible!

CAPTAIN JINKS. At any rate, here I am, and you won't get rid of me until I've straightened everything out. Ever since I left your room this afternoon I've been searching my brain and scouring the town for proof to show that I have done nothing dishonorable to you; to prove myself worthy at least of your—*respect*.

AURELIA. I do not ask for proofs, but I fear the *police* are not so lenient as a woman.

CAPTAIN JINKS [*surprised*]. *The police!*

AURELIA. Yes, the police! They've been here looking for you.

CAPTAIN JINKS. By George, I forgot! At two o'clock I was due. I'll tell you why the police want me—

AURELIA [*interrupting*]. Thank you, I don't care to know.

CAPTAIN JINKS. Is that honest?

AURELIA [*melting a little*]. No, it's *not* honest. Of course, I'm dying to know!

CAPTAIN JINKS. The day you landed I gave the Inspector a little bill to go easy with your trunks,

CAPTAIN JINKS

and he gave *me* in charge—that's all! Can't you forgive me if at two o'clock I thought of nothing except that I had lost your love?

AURELIA. Yes, I think I can forgive that—

A knock on the hall door.

CAPTAIN JINKS. Please don't answer it.

AURELIA. Come in!

PETER *backs into the room.*

CAPTAIN JINKS [*to* PETER]. What are you doing? Turn around!

PETER [*turning*]. That's what I call having tack! [*To* AURELIA.] Them same two lardy-dahs,—are you out as usual?

CAPTAIN JINKS. No. In!

AURELIA. Out!

CAPTAIN JINKS. In!

AURELIA [*half angry and half amused at his audacity*]. How dare you? Out!

CAPTAIN JINKS. In!

PETER. Yes, sir.

CAPTAIN JINKS. Show them up.

PETER. Yes, sir. [*He exits.*]

CAPTAIN JINKS. *I sent* for La Martine and Van Vorkenburg in your name.

CAPTAIN JINKS

AURELIA. *My name?* How dared you!

CAPTAIN JINKS. Oh, it did take a little pluck, but I've so much at stake I must try everything to win.

A knock on the hall door.

CAPTAIN JINKS. Come in.

CHARLIE *and* GUSSIE *enter.*

CHARLIE. You sent for us, Madame Trentoni?—

AURELIA. I did *not!* I wonder at your presumption in appearing here!

CHARLIE. No more presumption in *us* than in Jinks!

CAPTAIN JINKS. It was *I* who sent for you to come in Madame Trentoni's name.

CHARLIE. What in—what did you do that for?

CAPTAIN JINKS. Because it would be no use explaining about the cursed agreement and denying things behind your backs. I must do it before your faces and in her presence. I'm not afraid and not ashamed, because I will speak the truth!

CHARLIE. Good!

CAPTAIN JINKS. And I'm going to trust *you* to say what is *true*. I won't believe you two men would be willing to *lie* away the happiness and honor of any one, let alone an old friend.

CAPTAIN JINKS

CHARLIE. Certainly not.

CAPTAIN JINKS. You'll tell the truth about the wager affair?

CHARLIE. Of course.

CAPTAIN JINKS. And you, Gus?

GUSSIE. Why—yes.—

CAPTAIN JINKS. This bet then—did we make it *before we saw her?*

CHARLIE. I don't remember.

CAPTAIN JINKS. And didn't I repudiate it the minute I had seen this lady as an insult to her?

CHARLIE. No!

CAPTAIN JINKS. *What!*

CHARLIE. *No!*

CAPTAIN JINKS. Good evening. That's all I want out of you!

CHARLIE. What do you mean?

CAPTAIN JINKS [*calls*]. Peter!

PETER *enters and stands by the door.*

PETER. Yes, sir?

CAPTAIN JINKS. Show this gentleman out!

CHARLIE. Look here!

CAPTAIN JINKS [*interrupting strongly*]. Out!

CAPTAIN JINKS

CHARLIE *sneers and snaps open his "crush hat" into* Captain JINKS' *face, and exits, bowed out by* PETER.

CAPTAIN JINKS. Now, Gussie, what do you say? Wasn't that bet made before we'd seen Madame Trentoni?

GUSSIE. No!

CAPTAIN JINKS [*calls*]. Peter!

PETER [*by the door*]. Yes, sir?

CAPTAIN JINKS [*to* GUSSIE]. Good night! Quick, Peter, this gentleman's in a hurry!

GUSSIE *seizes a large bouquet which lies on the table and smashes it on the floor, and then exits, followed out by* PETER.

CAPTAIN JINKS. Jackasses! I sent for my friends hoping they would speak the truth and exonerate me. Now I must do without them. I did make that bet, but before I saw you.

AURELIA. But you *did make* the bet?

CAPTAIN JINKS. But before I'd seen you. *Before I'd seen you!* And then only as a joke. I've won your love honestly and I don't mean to lose it. I've waited until this evening should be over and your triumph won. The evening is over and your triumph is won! I've allowed Papa Belliarti to blackguard me, the old lady to flout me, *but now it's my turn, and you've got to believe in me!* I won't leave you till you do.

AURELIA [*reading his true nature in his face, and convinced by his manly sincerity, begins to decidedly relent*]. What was the old bet, anyway?

CAPTAIN JINKS. That I would get up a flirtation with you.

AURELIA. A flirtation? Is that all? But your friends said —

CAPTAIN JINKS. Oh, well, you know one's *friends* will say anything, and *such friends!*

AURELIA. And there was nothing about marriage in the bet?

CAPTAIN JINKS. No, nothing so serious as that, and I withdrew the foolish wager as soon as I had seen you.

AURELIA. Did I look so unpromising as all that?

CAPTAIN JINKS. And you meant it this morning when you told me you loved me; did n't you?

AURELIA [*softly*]. Yes.

CAPTAIN JINKS. On my soul, you can trust me with your happiness. Forgive me! You *must* forgive me, and *believe* in me.

AURELIA. Is that all?

CAPTAIN JINKS. No! And *love* me!

CAPTAIN JINKS

AURELIA. Oh!

CAPTAIN JINKS. Say it!

AURELIA. I forgive you, I believe in you, and— [*She hesitates.*]

CAPTAIN JINKS. And—

AURELIA. And—I—

A knock at the door and the Policeman *enters suddenly.*

THE POLICEMAN. Ah, ha! *There you are!* [*He stands and looks at* Captain JINKS *triumphantly.*]

Great consternation on the part of AURELIA *and* Captain JINKS.

THE POLICEMAN. I thought I'd catch you near the singing bird's cage!

AURELIA. No, no! [*Going to the* Policeman.] Mr. Policeman,—Captain Jinks *is n't here!*

THE POLICEMAN. Oh, is n't he, ma'am?

AURELIA [*very persuasively*]. *No! You* don't see him!—

THE POLICEMAN [*laughing*]. Oh, don't I?

AURELIA. Could n't you be just a *little nearsighted*, just to please *me?*—

THE POLICEMAN. Could n't be stone blind, ma'am! would n't be right.

CAPTAIN JINKS

CAPTAIN JINKS. I give you my word of honor I will appear in court the first thing to-morrow.

AURELIA. And I'll give you *my* word of honor, too. Now you *don't* see him here, *do you?*—

THE POLICEMAN. Meaning no disrespect to you, lady, I can't take his word for it. He skipped his bail!

AURELIA. But *my* word?

THE POLICEMAN. Sorry, but we learned a passage to Europe was taken in *your name to-night.* Now you're singing here all winter and have made a P. T. Barnum success, so that there passage can't be for *you*, and we've pretty well twigged to the little game!

AURELIA. Good gracious, what an idea! [*To* Captain JINKS.] Look here, let's tell him the truth!

CAPTAIN JINKS [*embarrassed*]. What?

AURELIA [*also embarrassed*]. Why—that I—that you—

CAPTAIN JINKS [*crossing to the* Policeman, *speaks desperately*]. I'm head over heels in love with her, officer, and that doesn't half express it—

AURELIA [*quickly following* Captain JINKS, *and taking his arm*]. And we had a quarrel this noon!

CAPTAIN JINKS [*quickly*]. I thought I'd lost her

and it drove everything else out of my mind!

AURELIA [*quickly*]. And I felt so beastly I took that passage and was going to sail to-morrow!

CAPTAIN JINKS. Do you believe us?

THE POLICEMAN. I'm thinking.—

CAPTAIN JINKS. Sh—he's thinking!

AURELIA. We've made it all up now, and we're going in there *where Mapleson* is. [*Pointing to the back room.*]

CAPTAIN JINKS. And if I'm with *him*, surely you can trust me!

AURELIA. And you have his word of honor. [*To Captain* JINKS.] Give him your hand. [Captain JINKS *does so.*]

CAPTAIN JINKS. And *her* word of honor!

AURELIA. Yes, sir! [*Putting her hand on* Captain JINKS' *and the* Policeman's. *The* Policeman *is very much embarrassed. They all separate.*] Do you see Captain Jinks NOW?

THE POLICEMAN [*after a look all about the room*]. *Not a sign of him!*

AURELIA. Oh, you darling! [*Seizing* PETER's *large horseshoe, she loads his arms with it, and he hurries out. She starts to go to* Captain JINKS, *but* Professor BELLIARTI *enters from the back room. She rushes to*

CAPTAIN JINKS

her foster-father and embraces him.] Those two men *lied* to you! You *must* believe in him—*I do!* [Professor BELLIARTI *comes slowly down the room.*]

CAPTAIN JINKS. I made no bet about marrying Madame Trentoni, sir. I did make a foolish wager before seeing her that I would flirt with her. After meeting your foster-daughter on the dock I realized the unworthiness of our wager, and I drew up that I O U to pay up as if I'd lost, so we might call it all off. *She's* forgiven me, *won't* you?

Professor BELLIARTI *looks him searchingly straight in the eyes.*

CAPTAIN JINKS [*hesitatingly—offering his cigar case*]. Have a cigar, sir?

Professor BELLIARTI *looks from one to the other, then takes a cigar graciously, and gives* Captain JINKS *his hand.*

PROFESSOR BELLIARTI. Thank you!—And I do gladly take that "blackguard" back!

AURELIA *starts to embrace him; he eludes her embrace, leaving* Captain JINKS' *arms to enfold her.*

PROFESSOR BELLIARTI [*opening the double doors at back*]. Ladies and gentlemen, the health and happiness of Captain Jinks and his promised bride.

As Professor BELLIARTI *gives the toast, all cry "Hooray!" and at the same moment* PETER *rushes*

CAPTAIN JINKS

in with his clothes half torn off his back, but with his horseshoe in his arms.

PETER. No, he did n't! Not my hor'shoe!

And as all the guests, having drunk the toast, begin to sing "Captain Jinks of the Horse Marines," AURELIA, *happy and proud on* Captain JINKS' *arm, goes to join her friends, and the curtain falls.*

THE END OF THE PLAY

BIBLIOLIFE

Old Books Deserve a New Life
www.bibliolife.com

Did you know that you can get most of our titles in our trademark **EasyScript**™ print format? **EasyScript**™ provides readers with a larger than average typeface, for a reading experience that's easier on the eyes.

Did you know that we have an ever-growing collection of books in many languages?

Order online:
www.bibliolife.com/store

Or to exclusively browse our **EasyScript**™ collection:
www.bibliogrande.com

At BiblioLife, we aim to make knowledge more accessible by making thousands of titles available to you – quickly and affordably.

Contact us:
BiblioLife
PO Box 21206
Charleston, SC 29413

LaVergne, TN USA
18 January 2010
170431LV00004B/19/P